JUNKERS Ju 87

STUKAGESCHWADER 1937-41

SERIES EDITOR: TONY HOLMES

OSPREY COMBAT AIRCRAFT • 1

JUNKERS Ju 87
STUKAGESCHWADER 1937-41

John Weal

OSPREY
AEROSPACE

First published in Great Britain in 1997
by Osprey, a division of Reed International Books,
Michelin House, 81 Fulham Road, London SW3 6RB
and Auckland, Melbourne

© 1997 Osprey Publishing
© 1997 Osprey Publishing/Aerospace Publishing Colour Side-views
Reprinted Autumn 1997

ISBN 1 85532 636 1

Edited by Tony Holmes
Page design by TT Designs, T & S Truscott

Cover Artwork by Iain Wyllie
Aircraft Profiles by John Weal
Figure Artwork by Mike Chappell
Scale Drawings by Mark Styling

Printed in Hong Kong

ACKNOWLEDGEMENTS
Both the author and the editor would like to thank Herr Holger Nauroth, John
Foreman, Dr Alfred Price, Robert Simpson and Aerospace Publishing for the
provision of photographs for inclusion in this volume. The author also
acknowledges that the Stuka crewmembers' accounts quoted in these pages are
translations by him from contemporary German records held in his collection.
Similarly, the editor has used brief quotes in chapter three from *Spitfire Pilot* by
Flt Lt D M Crook, DFC, (published by Faber and Faber in 1942) and *One of
the Few* by Gp Capt J A Kent, DFC and Bar, AFC, (published by William
Kimber in 1971).

EDITOR'S NOTE
To make this new series as authoritative as possible, the editor would be inter-
ested in hearing from any individual who may have relevant photographs, docu-
mentation or first-hand experiences relating to combat aircraft, and their crews,
of the various theatres of war. Any material used will be fully credited to its
original source. Please write to Tony Holmes at 1 Bradbourne Road, Sevenoaks,
Kent, TN13 3PZ, Great Britain.

Front cover
Flown by the *Staffelkapitan* of
5./StG 77, Ju 87B-1 'Anton-Nordpol'
(S2+AN) releases its full warload of a
single 250-kg bomb and four 50-kg
underwing bombs against a target in
the western Channel in the high
summer of 1940. Moments after
dropping its ordnance the Ju 87 was
set upon by a Hurricane I of Fighter
Command's No 10 Group and badly
shot up
(cover artwork by Iain Wyllie)

CONTENTS

PREPARING FOR WAR

When 2Lt William Henry Brown of No 84 Sqn, Royal Flying Corps (RFC), tilted the nose of his S.E.5a scout earthwards over the Western Front shortly after midday on 14 March 1918, little did he realise that he was setting in motion a train of ideas and events which would circle the globe, via the United States and the Far East, only to return to this very area to wreak havoc some 22 years later.

What made Harry Brown's little fighter so different from the hundreds of other S.E.5as patrolling the skies on that March day was that it had been fitted with a makeshift bomb-rack beneath the fuselage. And the German ammunition barge which he targeted and sank on the canal east of St Quentin that afternoon was fated to become the victim of arguably the world's first deliberate dive-bombing attack.

Despite this initial success, No 84 Sqn did not carry out any further missions of this kind; becoming noted instead for its sterling service as a ground-strafing unit. And although a series of carefully controlled tests – using both S.E.5a and Sopwith Camel fighters – were carried out at the RAE Armament Experimental Station at Orfordness on the Suffolk coast in the immediate post-Armistice months, the powers-that-be in the Royal Air Force (as the RFC had become on 1 April 1918) decided that any advantages to be gained from precision dive-bombing would be far outweighed by the inevitable heavy losses which could be expected among aircraft and trained pilots engaged in such attacks.

Most of the world's major land-based air forces were of a similar mind. At first, only the United States Naval and Marine Corps air arms championed the dive-bomber concept as offering the best chance of delivering the pinpoint accuracy required to hit small, moving targets at sea.

Meanwhile, in defeated Germany any arguments for or against the dive-bomber as opposed to the traditional high-altitude level bomber were perforce purely academic. Shorn of all offensive weaponry by the 1919 Treaty of Versailles, Germany's arms manufacturers were expressly forbidden from producing any replacements. Hardly was the ink dry on the hated *Diktat*, however, before companies began seeking ways to circumvent the strictures imposed upon them.

One such firm was the Dessau-based Junkers *Flugzeugwerke AG* which, in the early 1920s, set up Swedish subsidiary AB *Flygindustri* at Limhamn-Malmö. Here, they were free to concentrate on military, rather than civil, aircraft production and development. Among the types built at Limhamn was a highly advanced two-seat fighter. Designed by Dipl-Ing Karl Plauth and Hermann Pohlmann, the two Junkers K 47 prototypes,

Co-designer of the K 47, Dipl-Ing Hermann Pohlmannn (centre), served with the Imperial German Air Arm in Italy during World War 1. Shot down late in 1917, he became a prisoner of the British. He joined the Junkers company in 1923, and ten years later the then 39-year-old Pohlmann began work on arguably the most famous design of his entire career – the Junkers Ju 87

Equipped with a 480 hp Bristol Jupiter VII engine, the first prototype Junkers K 47 is here seen bearing its initial Swedish civil registration, S-AABW. After subsequent evaluation at Lipezk, this machine – re-engined with the 540 hp Siemens Sh 20 – was assigned to the DVL (German Aviation Experimenal Establishment) at Berlin-Adlersdorf as the Junkers A 48 dy, registration D-2012

which first flew in 1929, were subsequently evaluated at the clandestine German air training centre at Lipezk, north of Voronezh, in the Soviet Union.

And while a batch of 12 production K 47 fighters was completed in Sweden for export (six being supplied to the Chinese Central Government and four ultimately going to the Soviet Union), the *Reichswehr* (the 100,000 strong internal army grudgingly allowed Germany by the Versailles signatories) purchased the two prototypes, plus the two remaining export aircraft.

Found to be capable of carrying a 100-kg bomb-load (eight 12.5-kg fragmentation bombs) on their underwing struts, three of these machines were tested at Lipezk for their suitability in the dive-bombing role. Although successful, high unit costs precluded the tightly-budgeted *Reichswehr* from awarding a production contract, and the four aircraft (now designated as A 48s) served out their time in the *Reich* engaged in a variety of quasi-civil duties.

The seed had nevertheless been sown, and in the predatory shape of the original K 47 - despite the uncranked wing and twin tail unit - the embry-

Although the Heinkel He 50 failed miserably as an 'interim dive-bomber', the type was resurrected during the latter half of the war as a night ground-attack aircraft on the Eastern Front. This pair, pictured during the winter of 1943/44, belong to NSGr 11, a unit composed of Estonian volunteers

onic form of the wartime Stuka could already be seen emerging.

A further two aircraft were to play a part in the story of German dive-bomber development before the advent of the Junkers Ju 87, however. The first of these came about as a direct result of growing Japanese interest in dive-bombing. Although an erstwhile ally of the Western Powers during World War 1, Japan herself was now also restricted by international treaty in the number, and tonnage, of the capital ships she was permitted to build (a ratio of three-to-two in favour of the United States and Great Britain). Seeking ways to redress the balance, and keenly aware of the ongoing dive-bomber experiments being conducted by the US Navy across the Pacific, Japan turned to Germany for assistance, approaching not Junkers, but the reputable seaplane manufacturing firm of Ernst Heinkel AG.

The resulting two-seater biplane design stressed for diving, and initially equipped with floats, was later exported to Japan as the Heinkel He 50D, and served as the basis for the Imperial Japanese Navy's own Aichi D1A carrier-borne dive-bomber.

Heinkel then offered a second (landplane) prototype to the *Reichswehr*. After a demonstration at the Rechlin test centre in 1932, followed by trials at Lipezk, the type was accepted into service as the He 50A interim dive-bomber in 1933, the year that Adolf Hitler came to power. It was thus the *Reichswehr* under the aegis of the Weimar Republic, and not the new National Socialist regime, which was responsible for preparing the groundwork and introducing the dive-bomber into Germany's covert, but burgeoning, new armoury.

However, Hitler and the head of his still clandestine air force - one Hermann Göring - were more than willing to tread the path already laid down for them. And when World War 1 fighter ace turned international stunt pilot Ernst Udet came back from a tour of the United States in the early 1930s extolling the virtues and dive-bombing abilities of the Curtiss Hawk II fighter then being offered for export, Göring authorised the newly established *Reichsluftfahrtministerium* (German Air Ministry) to provide Udet with the necessary funds to purchase two examples of the type for use in his aerobatic displays. It was a shrewd move, for not only did it give German designers the opportunity to examine state-of-the-art American technology, but also acted as a bribe in tempting the 'freebooting' Udet (who had ended World War 1 in command of Jasta 4 of the *Jagdgeschwader* 'Richthofen' under Göring) back into the official Luftwaffe fold.

The dual-role capability of the Curtiss machines prompted the *Technisches Amt* (Technical Office) of the RLM to issue similar specifications in February 1934 for a single-seat fighter and dive-bomber. The winning design in the shape of the Henschel Hs 123 made its public debut at Berlin-Johannisthal in May of the following year. Flown by Ernst Udet himself, its performance did much to strengthen the hand of

Henschel's foray into dive-bomber production in the form of the Hs 123 is now better known for its long, and illustrious, service as a ground-attack aircraft – it too was still active on the Russian Front as late as 1944. This early example, Hs 123A-1 Wk-Nr 858, carries the markings of 3./StG 165, which operated the type between 1936 and 1938

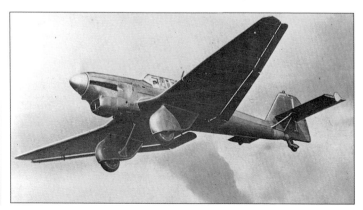

The first prototype Junkers Ju 87 V1 featured a twin-tail unit, but during a medium-angle test dive this assembly began to oscillate. When the pilot attempted to recover, the entire starboard vertical surface parted company with the rest of the tail section, causing the aircraft to crash

Consequently the next two prototypes, the V2 and V3 (pictured), were hastily redesigned with centrally-mounted fin and rudder assemblies

the pro-Stuka (i.e. dive-bomber) lobby within the RLM. Yet, if one discounts its early days in Spain, the Henschel was destined never to see action as such. Throughout the whole of its long operational career - it was still flying on the Eastern Front in 1944 - the *'eins-zwei-drei'*, or 'one-two-three', was employed to great effect as a low-level close-support aircraft. For despite being the first Stuka design to be ordered in any quantity for the Luftwaffe, the Hs 123 was regarded from the outset as a *'Sofortlösung'* – an 'immediate solution' or temporary measure – to bridge the gap until the second, and final, phase of the dive-bomber programme produced a more advanced two-seater machine offering an improved performance and heavier bomb-load.

To this end, the RLM turned back to Dipl-Ing Hermann Pohlmann of Junkers, co-designer of the original K 47 (Karl Plauth had lost his life in a flying accident before the K 47 was completed). Pohlmann had begun design work on the Ju 87 on his own initiative back in 1933 when the subject of a second phase to the *Sturzbomber-Programm* had first been broached. By the time the official specification was finally issued some two years later, he had already commenced the construction of three prototypes, leaving rival firms Arado and Heinkel well out of the running.

Although obviously a product of the same stable as the K 47, the early Ju 87s were, by contrast, particularly ugly and angular aircraft, characterised by the inverted gull wing which would be the hallmark of every one of the 5700+ Stukas built. But the Ju 87 had been designed to fulfil a specific role, and in this it was unsurpassed, even if (when it was in its natural element swooping almost vertically on its intended target) it was likened somewhat fancifully to an evil bird of prey – 'its radiator bath and fixed, spatted, undercarriage resembled gaping jaws and extended talons'.

The first prototype Ju 87 V1, powered by a Rolls-Royce Kestrel V 12-cylinder, upright-Vee, liquid-cooled, engine, featured a twin-tail

unit not dissimilar to that of its K 47 predecessor. But when this failed in flight during a medium-angle test dive, causing the V1 to crash, the remaining prototypes were redesigned with a centrally-mounted single fin and rudder assembly.

A fourth prototype was later added to the first three, this, the Ju 87 V4, incorporating all the lessons learned from flight-testing the original trio. With its Junkers Jumo 210Aa inverted-Vee engine in a revised, lowered, cowling to improve forward visibility, re-contoured cockpit canopy and enlarged vertical tail surfaces, the V4 led directly to the first batch of fully-armed Ju 87A-0 pre-production models which started coming off the assembly line before the end of 1936. These in turn were followed during the course of 1937 by the A-1 and A-2 production runs, the latter being equipped with the uprated Jumo 210Da engine.

In 1938, hard on the heels of the last 'Anton' to be built, there appeared the first of the 'Bertas'. When compared to the Ju 87A, the B-model featured not just a more powerful Jumo 211 engine with direct fuel injection, but a completely redesigned and reconstructed fuselage, cockpit and vertical tail. The most striking difference between the two, however, was the abandonment of the 'Anton's' huge 'trousered' undercarriage in favour of the slightly less obtrusive, and therefore aerodynamically cleaner, spatted leg.

By the outbreak of World War 2, the Ju 87A had already been withdrawn from first-line service and relegated to training units. On the open-

These two shots of an *'Anton'* and a *'Berta'* – taken from similar angles – clearly illustrate the major external differences between the two. Note the former's smooth upper nose contours, neat rectangular radiator intake, huge trousered and braced undercarriage and hinged-section cockpit canopy with twin aerial mast 'horns'. In contrast, the *'Berta's'* upper cowling is 'stepped' to accommodate the oil cooler intake, whilst the rounded chin radiator is altogether larger and more obtrusive. The new spatted undercarriage may be an aerodynamic improvement, but the same can hardly be said of the sliding-section canopy, with its redesigned rear-gunner's position. The white sidewall tyres of the trolley/hoist being used to lift the bomb on to the *'Anton's'* ventral cradle are a nice touch for modellers. In the meantime the *'Berta's'* groundcrew appear to be having some difficulty with that starting handle

This *'Anton'* of *Stuka Vorschule* 1 (Dive Bomber Preliminary School 1) was still in service as a trainer at Bad Aibling in the winter of 1940-41 – a fact indicated by the large numeral forward of the fuselage four-letter code and the post-1939 pattern and presentation of the national insignia. Note too the name *'Irene'* on the cowling, inspired by the girlfriend of pilot-instructor August Diemer, and the removal of the lower sections of the under-carriage trousers to prevent a build-up of compacted snow

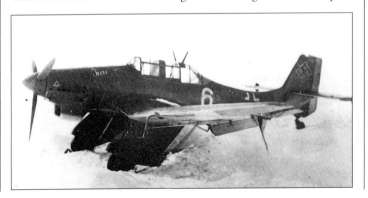

ing morning of hostilities the Luftwaffe's operational Stuka force, composed almost entirely of early Ju 87Bs, numbered exactly 346, of which all but 22 were serviceable.

The weapon had thus been forged. But what of the units specially created to fight and fly this latest, and as-yet untried, addition to the *Reich's* aerial inventory . . .

UNITS ARE FORMED

As was perhaps to be expected with the activation of an entirely new arm which had no World War 1 experience to fall back on, the early days of the *Stukawaffe* were beset with no few difficulties. Indeed, the confusing welter of re-designations and reorganisation which marked its gestation would carry over into the war years, and only attain some semblance of order late in 1943 when, ironically, the term 'Stuka' was dropped and the remaining units re-mustered as *Schlachtgeschwader*. Throughout their existence, the *Stukagruppen*, more than any other, would suffer from the Luftwaffe's penchant for shuffling and redesignating its component formations. The first *Stukagruppe* of all, for example (created in 1935), would serve under six different identities before its final surrender some ten years later – *Fliegergruppe* Schwerin (1934-36), I./StG 162 (1936-37), IV.(St)/LG 1 (1937-42), I./StG 5 (1942-43), I./StG 1 (1943), I./SG 1 (1943-45)!

It all started simply enough, however. On 1 April 1934 the first unit of the new *Reichsluftwaffe*, a three-*Staffel* strong fighter wing equipped with the Arado Ar 65, was formally activated under the designation *Fliegergruppe* Döberitz. This initial form of nomenclature, using only the generic title *Fliegergruppe* (Air Wing) together with the name of the home base, was specifically chosen to afford no clue as to a unit's function (i.e. whether bomber or fighter), or as to its place within the overall framework of the new Luftwaffe.

Within weeks of its creation, *Fliegergruppe* Döberitz was tasked with training a cadre of pilots for the first *Stukagruppe* (orders for which had been issued some six months earlier in October 1933). This came into being in the late summer of 1934 as the *Fliegergruppe* Schwerin. At first flying the fighter types on which its pilots had trained (primarily the Ar 65 and Heinkel He 51), the *Gruppe* subsequently accepted delivery of its first 12 He 50 interim dive-bombers – another 24 were taken on charge the following year.

On 3 April 1935 *Fliegergruppe* Schwerin received the honorary title 'Immelmann', which its descendants would carry throughout the war. Early in 1936 the unit reverted to the He 51 fighter, as the He 50 had proven completely unsuited for the dive-bombing role – the latter's offensive weaponry comprised just five 10 kg bombs, which was exactly half the bomb-load of the 1929-vintage K 47! The He 51s would be retained until the arrival of the first Henschel Hs 123s in the autumn.

Pre-war manoeuvres. A pair of *'Antons'* overfly a column of SdKfz 221 armoured cars advancing along a dusty country road in the summer of 1937

A pristine Ju 87A-1 of I./StG 167 sits securely anchored while awaiting its next mission. The fairing for the single fixed forward-firing machine-gun is clearly visible in the leading edge of the starboard wing. Note, however, that what appears to be a segment of dark camouflage on the rudder is in reality the warning pennant hanging from the locking device attached to the starboard outer aileron/flap section. This machine wears the standard tail marking of the period – a red band with white circle and black swastika superimposed

It was shortly after this re-equipment that the Luftwaffe discarded the term *Fliegergruppe* in favour of a new three-figure system of *Geschwader* designation. These three digits indicated, in sequence; (a) the unit's seniority within its own particular command area; (b) the type of unit (dive-bombers were coded '6'); and (c) the identity of the command area. *Fliegergruppe* Schwerin's new designation of I./StG 162 thus identified it in full to those in the know as the first *Gruppe* (I.) of the first *Geschwader* (1) of dive-bombers (6) to be established within the *Luftkreis* II (2) Berlin area of command.

On 7 March 1936 the *Third Reich* exercised its newly found military muscle for the first time by occupying the demilitarised zone of the Rhineland. I./StG 162 had prepared for its part in this earliest example of 'Hitlerian sabre-rattling' by detaching a number of pilots to Kitzingen, where they formed the nucleus of a second *Stukagruppe*, I./StG 165. This was then hastily transferred to the Frankfurt/Main and Mannheim areas to be closer to the scene of any Anglo-French counter-moves. Fortunately none came, for neither the weakened I./StG 162 nor the largely inexperienced I./StG 165 would have been able to offer any serious opposition had the Führer's bluff been called.

The pilots of this *Kette* of Ju 87As of II./StG 165 display their respective flying skills with a perfect echelon formation. The revised tail markings – with red band and white disc deleted but with the swastika still overlapping both fin and rudder – date this shot as early 1939. Close inspection will also reveal that the far machine, '52+F24', wears a reversed-colour camouflage pattern

The following month saw the activation of II./StG 162 at Lübeck-Blankensee on Ar 65s and He 50s. It would be another year before *Stukageschwader* 162 'Immelmann' was brought up to full establishment with the creation of III./StG 162 at Anklam on 15 March 1937 – by which time I. *Gruppe* had already relinquished its Hs 123s for the first examples of the Junkers Ju 87A-1.

Charged with working up the new two-seater aircraft for service, and with the development of effective operational dive-bombing tactics, the pilots of I./StG 162 also indulged in some highly illegal low-level flying practice. Completely ignoring the 50-metre minimum altitude rule, it became a matter of principle to leave wheel tracks from the fixed undercarriage across the surface of any field of standing crops they overflew! High-tension cables and the like would be nonchalantly leapfrogged at the very last moment. It was also standard procedure to approach every tree from below crown height, waiting again until the last second before lifting one wing to clear the obstacle. Just what the rearward-facing gunners thought of all this – suddenly seeing leaves and branches flash by at shoulder level – is not recorded.

One worthy who misjudged his height and bellied in during just such an escapade was confined to barracks for three days – reportedly not so much for either wiping off his undercarriage or presenting the local inhabitants with an opportunity to inspect and photograph the Ju 87, which was still very much on the secret list, but for cycling from the crash site to the nearest village while improperly dressed . . . he wasn't wearing his uniform jacket!

In July 1937 I./StG 162's activities were put on a more formal basis with their incorporation into *Lehrgeschwader* 1 as that organisation's dedicated dive-bombing component. The *Lehrgeschwader* (Operational Instruction and Evaluation Group) was a mixed formation unit, each of whose *Gruppen* were engaged in perfecting the tactics and proper operational usage of a specific aircraft type. Transferring from Schwerin to Barth on the Baltic coast, I./StG 162 would henceforth operate their Ju 87s as IV.(St)/LG 1.

II. and III./StG 162 were also both redesignated during the course of 1937. In May II.*Gruppe* had become I./StG 167. Initially remaining in Lübeck-Blankensee, they moved down to Austria the following year, taking up quarters at Graz concurrent with yet another change of identity as I./StG 168. Meanwhile, in October of the same year III./StG 162's Ju 87s had transferred to Breslau-Schöngarten

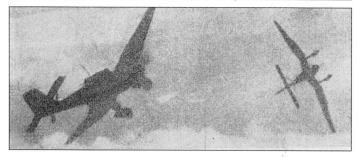

Although of poor quality, this sequence of stills from a German newsreel graphically illustrates the Stuka's classic wingover manoeuvre at the start of the dive

under their new guise of I./StG 163. The latter's redesignation was simply an administrative result of their moving into a different command area (*Luftkreis* III Dresden), as all they were doing was filling the vacant I.*Gruppe* slot of the 'Immelmann' *Geschwader* left by I./StG 162's departure in July.

The Luftwaffe's expansion programme of 1937 did see two completely new *Stukagruppen* activated, however, when I./StG 165 (the unit hur-

An alternative method of attack was for the individual *Ketten* to dive in vics of three as depicted here. In practice, however, the aircraft would normally be spaced further apart, with some 30 metres between each machine

As the threat of war loomed larger, the Stukas continued to hone their skills. A pair of *'Bertas'* offer low-level support as a Panzer II emerges from the tree-line and prepares to cross a patch of open ground . . .

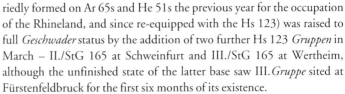

riedly formed on Ar 65s and He 51s the previous year for the occupation of the Rhineland, and since re-equipped with the Hs 123) was raised to full *Geschwader* status by the addition of two further Hs 123 *Gruppen* in March – II./StG 165 at Schweinfurt and III./StG 165 at Wertheim, although the unfinished state of the latter base saw III.*Gruppe* sited at Fürstenfeldbruck for the first six months of its existence.

Indeed, it was elements of *Stukageschwader* 165 which provided the dive-bomber presence during Hitler's next venture into territorial expansion – the near-bloodless annexation of Austria in March 1938. Total *Wehrmacht* fatalities during the operation totalled just 25, all of them the result of accidents.

In September of that same year all six existing *Stukagruppen* participated in the build-up of forces being assembled to add weight to the Führer's demands for the incorporation of the Sudeten territories of Czechoslovakia into the *Reich*. Four of the six (I./StG 163, I. and II./StG 165 and I./StG 168) were now equipped with the Ju 87A. Only III./StG 165 was still flying the He 123, while IV.(St)/LG 1 - as befitted its role as the unit responsible for evaluating the latest dive-bombing tactics - was already operating the new Ju 87B. In addition, five temporary *Fliegergruppen* (three of Hs 123s and two of He 54s) had also been specially activated.

This blatant assemblage of air power served its purpose, for the hastily-convened Munich conference of Western and Axis leaders resulted in the former's total acceptance of Hitler's demands. On 1 October 1938 German troops marched unopposed through the Czech border defences as if part of a military parade.

Shortly thereafter the three Hs 123-equipped *Fliegergruppen* were redesignated and incorporated into the *Stukawaffe* proper, *Fliegergruppe* 10 moving up to Insterburg in East Prussia as I./StG 160, *Fliegergruppe* 30 assuming the mantle of a new I./StG 162 at Jever and *Fliegergruppe* 50 taking up residence at Grottkau, some 50 km south-east of Breslau in Silesia, as II./StG 163 'Immelmann'. The Luftwaffe's Stuka arm had thereby reached its peak strength of nine *Gruppen* with which it would embark upon World War 2 less than 12 months later – albeit not without undergoing yet more redesignations in the interim!

One final unit remains to be mentioned, however. On the day Germany occupied the Sudetenland a single *Stukastaffel* had been activated at Kiel-Holtenau. This was a naval squadron intended for service aboard the as-yet unfinished aircraft carrier *Graf Zeppelin*. Initially equipped with Ju 87As, 4.(St)/TrGr 186 (*Trägergruppe* = carrier wing) spent the following months practising dummy deck-landings at Travemünde while waiting delivery of the Ju 87C-0, a special navalised version of the '*Berta*' complete with folding wings, jettisonable main

. . . while here on the bombing ranges a steeply diving *'Anton'* attacks the hulk of what appears to be an ex-Czech tank

The first real test came in Spain. Previous assertions that the machine illustrated here is '29.1' – the single Ju 87A-0 sent to Spain in November 1936 – would seem to be disproved by the presence of another Ju 87 alongside it ('29.1' was reportedly returned to the Reich several months before the arrival of the 'Jolanthe' *Kette* in mid-January 1938). It would point too to the latter's using another badge, described by one source as an 'umbrella superimposed on a derby hat' (a tongue-in-cheek reference to their 'civilian' status while en route to Spain), before they adopted the famous pink pig

undercarriage members (for emergency landings on water), flotation equipment, catapult spools and arrester hook.

While they were thus engaged, and the other nine *Gruppen* divided their time between perfecting their dive-bombing techniques and parading their growing might as a backdrop to the Führer's political ambitions, the Ju 87 Stuka had, in fact, already undergone its baptism of fire far beyond the borders of the *Reich*.

CONDOR LEGION

On the night of 1 August 1936 the steamship *Usaramo* had slipped quietly out of Hamburg harbour. At first light some five days later she docked at Cadiz, in southern Spain, and began discharging her cargo. This included six crated He 51s, twenty 20 mm anti-aircraft pieces, some 100 tons of additional war material and 86 thinly-disguised civil 'tourists'. Although subjected to several salvoes from an offshore Spanish Republican destroyer, all was landed safely. The *Usaramo* had been carrying as 'cargo' some of the first participants of *Unternehmen 'Zauberfeuer'* (Operation *Magic Fire*), Hitler's response to the appeal for help from Gen Franco, head of the Nationalist coup against the Spanish Government which had been launched from Spanish Morocco less than three weeks earlier.

After landing, the men and supplies were immediately ferried to Nationalist-held Seville, meeting up at the town's Tablada airfield with ten Ju 52 transports flown in directly from Germany by captains and crews of the state airline Lufthansa. The build-up of the *Condor Legion* had begun.

As part of a later shipment in November, the contents of one crate also convoyed to Tablada for assembly was surrounded by the utmost secrecy. This was a single machine plucked from the pre-production batch of Ju 87A-0s freshly rolled off the Dessau assembly line. Allocated the military serial 29-1 and piloted by Unteroffizier Hermann Beuer, it was assigned to VJ/88, the experimental *Staffel* of the *Legion's* fighter wing which comprised not only three prototype Bf 109s and a cannon-armed prototype of the He 112, but also a trio of Hs 123s which had arrived some weeks earlier.

Little is known of 29-1's subsequent career in Spain, other than that it transferred with VJ/88 from Tablada up to Vitoria, in northern Castile, in February 1937 to take part in the Nationalist offensive against Bilbao. It was reportedly still at Vitoria some five months later but, shrouded in secrecy to the end, is presumed to have been shipped back to the *Reich* from one of the newly-captured Spanish Biscay ports shortly thereafter.

In mid-January 1938 three Ju 87A-1s arrived at Vitoria, these machines hailing from IV.(St)/LG 1's 11.*Staffel* based at Barth. Now coded 29-2, -3 and -4 (and initially

piloted by Unteroffizier Ernst Bartels and Oberleutnante Gerhard Weyert and Hermann Haas respectively), they were officially incorporated into the *Legion* as the fighter wing's fifth *Staffel* (5.J/88), but became universally known as the 'Jolanthe' *Kette* after their unit badge. This depicted a large pink sow, and could trace its origins back to Barth, where the *Gruppenkommandeur* of IV.(St)/LG 1, Oberstleutnant Günther Schwartzkopff (one of the most fervent supporters of the Stuka concept) had nicknamed the Ju 87 after the eponymous heroine of a favourite film comedy of the day that centred around a pig – *'Krach um Jolanthe'* ('Trouble with Iolanthe')!

On 7 February the *Kette* moved up to Calamocha, this barren sandy field south of Zaragoza serving as J/88's major base during the battle of Teruel. And it was here that the Ju 87s began to put into operational practice what up till now had only been theory. One of the first things they discovered was that the *'Anton's'* trousered undercarriage did not like Calamocha's soft surface, and that take-offs and landings were much easier if the wheel fairings were removed – a portent of Russian spring mud four years hence! It was also found that the Ju 87A's 500-kg bomb-load could only be carried if the rear cockpit seat was empty. The normal offensive load in Spain therefore had to be restricted to a 250-kg bomb.

During the latter half of March the *Kette* undertook a number of precision dive-bombing attacks on bridges and other targets as Republican forces retreated across Aragon – not always with the desired results, it must be admitted. In these early days near misses nearly always outnumbered direct hits by a substantial margin, but they were learning their trade nonetheless. And as new crews from the homeland replaced the original trio on a rotational basis, a steady stream of returnees to the *Reich* were taking back with them an invaluable pool of practical experience.

Transferring forward to La Cenia, the *'Antons'* supported both the advance on Valencia and the subsequent breakthrough to the Mediter-

And here is 'Jolanthe' in all her glory on the port undercarriage trouser of a bombed-up *'Anton'*. But this machine poses another puzzle as all references are adamant that only three Ju 87A-1s served with the *Condor Legion*, yet this *'Anton'* clearly displays the individual number '5'! Was a fourth aircraft sent to replace a hitherto unrecorded loss among the original trio, were the *Kette's* numbers altered at intervals to confuse the enemy, or is this simply a machine painted up for propaganda purposes?

A massed take-off by the *Legion's* entire Stuka arm! All three A-1s of the 'Jolanthe' *Kette* kick up dust as they gather speed across Calamocha's sandy surface

ranean coast. Following this run of Nationalist successes, they more than proved their worth during the Republican counter-offensive along the Ebro late in July. On the 27th alone, the trio mounted no fewer than four separate attacks on enemy troop concentrations and crossing points south of Mequinenza. With the Republicans finally broken once and for all, the way was left open for the final push through Catalonia to the French border. But the 'Iolanthe' *Kette* did not witness the end, for after several attacks on shipping in Tarragona and other ports along the Mediterranean, the three war-weary *'Antons'* were quietly returned to Germany in October 1938.

They were replaced in Spain by five Ju 87B-1s, but so effective had their predecessors been that the newcomers found little to do. Capable of carrying a full 500-kg bomb-load, they were attached, more fittingly, to 5.K/88 – the fifth *Staffel* of the *Legion*'s bomber wing. During the closing weeks of the Catalonian offensive they sometimes accompanied larger formations of He 111s attacking enemy positions. The *'Bertas'* also saw limited action on the Madrid front in mid-March 1939, but were no longer present to participate in the great victory display and flypast that was staged some two months later. Crated up, they were spirited out of Spain as quietly and unobtrusively as the single Ju 87A-0 had been smuggled in some 30 months earlier.

The experience gained from the handful of Stukas sent to participate in the Spanish Civil War was indeed invaluable. Air and groundcrews alike practised and perfected their skills and techniques, equipment was honed and numerous modifications made. But one ingredient had been lacking – serious opposition. In the air the Ju 87s enjoyed strong

With full bomb loads, a *Kette* of 'Bertas' head for a Republican target. Another shot for the markings 'buffs', this photo shows the leader's aircraft wearing the codes '29.11'. This would seem to indicate that the five B-1s sent to Spain were not numbered sequentially with the four (or five?) original 'Antons'

Although no Ju 87s were lost in Spain, not all returned unscathed. This exit hole in the port tailplane of an unidentified *'Berta'* is evidence of the unwelcome attentions of Republican anti-aircraft gunners

fighter protection, whilst effective Republican anti-aircraft fire was almost non-existent except in the immediate vicinity of those targets deemed to be vitally important.

A great feeling of confidence in the dive-bomber had therefore been engendered by the Stuka's performance in Spain. No bad thing, and one which would serve the crews well in the opening months of the war that was to come. However, in one important respect the Ju 87 remained untested – its ability to survive in a completely hostile airspace.

Meanwhile, what of the nine *Stukagruppen* which had remained in the *Reich*? On 1 May they underwent a major round of redesignations when the somewhat cumbersome three-figure system of unit identification was replaced by a simpler block format based upon the four existing *Luftflotten* (Air Fleets, or territorial commands). *Luftflotten* 1 to 4 were assigned identity blocks 1-25, 26-50, 51-75 and 76-100 respectively. Just how this affected the *Stukawaffe* is best illustrated by the following table:

Luftflotte 1:	I./StG 160	became I./StG 1
	I./StG 163	became I./StG 2 'Immelmann'
	II./StG 163	became III./StG 2 'Immelmann'
Luftflotte 2:	I./StG 162	became I./StG 26
Luftflotte 3:	I./StG 165	became I./StG 51
	II./StG 165	became II./StG 51
	III./StG 165	became III./StG 51
Luftflotte 4:	I./StG 168	became I./StG 76.

It will be seen from the above that IV.(St)/LG 1 and the naval 4.(St)/TrGr 186 were not part of these changes, but two further alterations did take place. Firstly, *Luftflotte* 2 lost its sole *Stukagruppe* almost immediately when I./StG 26 was redesignated II./StG 2 – although thus nominally a part of *Stukageschwader* 'Immelmann', this II.*Gruppe* was never subordinated to its parent *Geschwader* as such, remaining instead a semi-autonomous unit until its eventual incorporation into StG 3 early in 1942. And secondly, *Luftflotte* 3 likewise relinquished two of its three assigned *Stukagruppen* when I. and II./StG 51 were transferred to neighbouring *Luftflotte* 4 as I. and II./StG 77. These then were the final designations (for the time being!) of the Luftwaffe's Stuka arm as all units gathered along the *Reich*'s eastern borders in preparation for the invasion of Poland (see the appendices for the Order of Battle of 1 September 1939).

One *Gruppe* was destined to suffer a grievous blow even before the first shots were fired. Hauptmann Walter Sigel's I./StG 76 had moved up from their peace-time base at Graz to Cottbus in Brandenburg.

One of the most colourful of all pre-war Stukas was this shark-mouthed B-1, purportedly flown by later Knight's Cross winner Major Alfons Orthofer of II./StG 77

Indicative of the conditions faced by Hauptmann Sigel and his I./StG 76 over Neuhammer, a pair of Stukas dive down into a seemingly solid blanket of cloud below

On 15 August they were scheduled to demonstrate the Stuka's abilities by staging a dummy dive-bombing attack for the benefit of visiting Luftwaffe generals at the Neuhammer training grounds on Sagan heath. Weather reconnaissance had reported seven-tenths cloud, rising to 2000 metres, over the target area, with perfect ground visibility below the 900 metre cloud base. Each loaded with cement practice bombs fitted with smoke flares, the Ju 87s would therefore approach at 4000 metres, dive through the cloud layer and release at 500 metres.

Sigel himself led the *Stabskette* (HQ flight) to the target zone, his adjutant and technical officer to left and right of him, and with the three *Staffeln* in close formation astern. As they had practised a hundred times before, Sigel tipped onto one wing to lead the *Gruppe* in a screaming power-dive towards the spectators hidden below.

The 10-15 seconds it would take to get through the cloud layer seemed interminable for the crews ensconced in their diving Stukas. But instead of slowly lightening, the milky-white haze in front of Sigel's windscreen grew suddenly darker – he was only 100 metres from the ground, with the entire *Gruppe* in faithful attendance behind him! *'Pull up - pull up - ground-mist!'*

The *Kommandeur* instinctively yanked on the stick, willing the Stuka out of its terminal plunge. Levelling out - according to some eyewitnesses, its wheels only two metres off the ground - Sigel's Ju 87 raced towards the woods bordering the target area, a fire-break cleared through the trees being his salvation. Aiming directly for the long green tunnel, the shaken Sigel slowly and carefully began to gain height.

His two wingmen were not so fortunate. As Sigel had pulled out (and almost 'blacked out' in the process), he had become dimly aware of his adjutant's machine smashing into the woods alongside him, and of the technical officer's aircraft exploding in a ball of flame. Behind them, all nine Stukas of the leading 2.*Staffel* slammed into the ground. Next in line, 3.*Staffel* broke in all directions as they sought desperately to recover. Most made it, but two pilots pulled up into involuntary loops and crashed on their backs in the trees.

Only 1.*Staffel*, whose *Kapitän*, Oberleutnant Dieter Peltz, would later rise to the position of *General der Kampfflieger* (GOC Bomber Forces), escaped unscathed. Having just initiated their dive, they quickly climbed back up out of the clouds. Circling, they watched in disbelief as one dirty brown column of smoke after another oozed from the white blanket below and spiralled up into the summer sky.

An enquiry into the loss of the 13 Stukas, and all 26 crew members, was held that same day. No blame was attached to Hauptmann Sigel, the cause of the catastrophe being the sudden, and unexpected, ground-mist which had become trapped below the cloud layer. This had effectively reduced the latter's base from the 900 metres reported by the met flight to just 100 metres by the time I./StG 76 arrived overhead some 60 minutes later.

The *Gruppe's* losses were immediately made good by the transfer of men and machines in from other units. Little more than a fortnight later Walter Sigel was leading the reconstituted I./StG 76 in action against live targets in Poland. The tragedy of Neuhammer had not been forgotten, however, rather simply overtaken by events even more cataclysmic.

THE *BLITZKRIEG* ERA

I t was no accident that the Ju 87 was selected to carry out the very first operation of World War 2, which was initiated some 20 minutes before the official outbreak of hostilities! Given the nature of the objective, no other choice was possible.

The easternmost province of the *Reich*, East Prussia, was cut off from Germany proper by the Polish Corridor. This hotly disputed strip of territory, which afforded the landlocked Poles access to the Baltic Sea, was another product of the Treaty of Versailles, and a contributory factor in Hitler's decision to attack Poland. Across its neck ran a single railway which connected the province to Berlin. This track would be a vital lifeline between the two in time of war. Its weakest link was the bridge at Dirschau (Tczew), where it spanned the River Vistula. Both Germans and Poles were aware of this, and the latter had prepared the bridge for demolition should they be attacked.

The target for the first bombing raid of the war was therefore not the bridge itself, but the demolition ignition points situated in blockhouses at nearby Dirschau station, plus the cables which ran out along the railway embankment on to the bridge. The objective was to prevent the structure from being destroyed before it could be seized by German ground troops being transported into Poland by armoured train. It was a job that only the Stuka could do.

Wearing civilian clothes, pilots of I./StG 1 – the unit ordered to carry out the attack – had undertaken their own first-hand reconnaissance by travelling back and forth several times in the sealed trains (inevitably known as 'corridor trains') in which Germans were allowed to traverse the

Ju 87B-1 'A5+DH' of I./StG 1, the *Gruppe* which carried out the first bombing raid of World War 2 . . .

100-km stretch of line that connected East Prussia with the Fatherland.

At exactly 04.26 hours on 1 September 1939 a *Kette* of Ju 87s of 3./StG 1, led by *Staffelkapitän* Oberleutnant Bruno Dilley, lifted off from their forward base in East Prussia for the eight-minute flight to the target. Despite the all-pervading ground-mist which blanketed the area, the trio of Stukas, each loaded with one 250-kg bomb, plus four smaller 50-kg weapons slung in

... and the target of that mission, the railway station at Dirschau (Tczew) in the Polish Corridor. Note one of the blockhouses in the left foreground which protected the ignition points for the demolition cables running out to the bridge (just visible in the background to the right of the ruined station building) carrying the railway over the River Vistula

The wrecked spans of the bridge which were destroyed by Polish army engineers before the arrival of German troops. Both this and the preceding photograph were taken after the area was finally occupied

pairs under each wing, soon spotted the unmistakable iron lattice-work of the bridge looming ahead of them. Flying at a height of just ten metres above the flat Vistula plain, the three pilots climbed as one before separating to plant their bombs unerringly on the station blockhouses, severing the finger-thick cables. Despite successfully completing their mission, it was all to no avail. The armoured train was delayed, and the Poles managed to destroy the bridge before German ground troops could reach it.

The first bombing raid of the war had been a carefully planned – albeit ultimately abortive – operation. That the Ju 87 could also lay claim to the first aerial victory of World War 2 came about quite by chance.

Elements of I./StG 2 'Immelmann' from Nieder-Ellguth in Upper Silesia had taken part in an early morning mixed-formation bombing raid on the Polish airfield at Krakow, but they had arrived at their target to

An impressive line-up of Ju 87B-2s of I./StG 2 'Immelmann' each bearing the *Gruppe's* distinctive Scottie-dog emblem, in the case of 1.*Staffel* - as here - on a white disc

A heavy ground mist covered much of the Baltic coastal provinces during the early hours of the opening morning of hostilities. Here, fully armed machines of the *Geschwaderstab* StG 2 'Immelmann' ('T6+CA' foreground) still await the first mission of the day among bombs already placed in position for their return and rearming for a second sortie

find it deserted – most Polish Air Force units vacated their peacetime bases and dispersed to prearranged, carefully concealed, satellite fields in the hours leading up to the invasion. Whilst returning from Krakow after dropping their ordnance on empty hangars, a gaggle of Stukas happened to overfly one such field near the village of Balice just as a pair of PZL P.11c fighters of No 121 Sqn were scrambling. Still clawing for altitude, but already intent on destroying one of the Ju 87s up ahead, the leader of the pair, Capt Mieczyslaw Medwecki (the CO of No 121), failed to spot another trio of Stukas closing up behind him. It took barely a few seconds for *Kettenführer* Leutnant Frank Neubert to overhaul the unwitting Polish pilot and then line up his wing guns. His aim was good, for his burst of fire hit the fighter's cockpit and caused Medwecki's PZL to 'suddenly explode in mid-air, bursting apart like a huge fireball – the fragments literally flew around our ears'.

As well as attempting to wipe out the Polish Air Force on the ground, Luftwaffe planners also targeted the small, but modern, Polish Navy. Not surprisingly, the naval 4.(St)/TrGr 186 was heavily involved in these attacks. The widespread mist over the coastal regions on the opening morning of the war thwarted the *Staffel's* first planned raid on Westerplatte, but conditions had improved enough by the afternoon for a second mission to be mounted against Hela. Approaching at 7000 metres, the four *Ketten* winged over into their dive. However, unlike targets in Spain, or the bridge over the River Vistula, the tiny harbour and naval strongpoint at Hela (situated at the very tip of the long, slender, peninsula of the same name) was defended by one of the biggest anti-aircraft batteries in all of Poland. Bracketed by fire as they plummeted from 5500 down to 700 metres, the Stukas lost two of their number in this, their very first engagement. In fact Hela, although under constant attack from land, sea

and air, would resist until the very end. Its beleaguered defenders did not surrender until 1 October, some four days after Warsaw had fallen. Subsequent German investigations revealed that 4.(St)/TrGr 186's initial attack must have been launched in the face of some 250 individual anti-aircraft barrels!

On 3 September the *Staffel* hit the main Polish naval base at Gdingen (Gdynia), where they sank the 1540-ton destroyer *Wicher* and badly damaged the minelayer *Gryf.* However, despite destroying numerous other coastal targets, time

Crewmen inspect flak damage to the tailplane and rear fuselage of an unidentified *'Berta'* after a mission over Poland

The 2227-ton Polish minelayer *Gryf* settled on the bottom of Gdingen (Gdynia) harbour after the attack by 4.(St)/TrGr 186 on 3 September 1939

and again the unit returned to Hela. *Staffelkapitän* Hauptmann Blattner, an ex-transatlantic captain with Lufthansa, described one such raid;

'Three minutes after the orders for the attack were received we were in the air. We climbed away from our base (Stolp-West, on the German side of the Corridor) and had reached our normal operating height of 7000 metres by the time we crossed the coast at Rixhöft. I led the *Staffel* in a wide arc out to sea, intending to approach the tip of Hela out of the sun from the east.

'I could see little through the broken cloud below, but over on our right another *Gruppe* (IV.(St)/LG 1) on its way to Gdingen was catching heavy flak. Then it was our turn. My observer called out the positions of the shell bursts, some 100 to 150 metres away from us, as we neared the objective.

'All thoughts of the flak were driven from my mind as I led the *Staffel* down in a steep dive. Despite the apparent confusion, each aircraft was aiming at a pre-assigned target. Our weeks of training against the old *Hessen* (a 13,000-ton turn of the century battleship, rebuilt as a radio-controlled target ship in 1936-37) had not been wasted!'

It was also while attacking Hela that another of the *Staffel's* Ju 87C-0s was severely damaged by anti-aircraft fire. Its pilot actuated the explosive bolts which jettisoned the main undercarriage preparatory to ditching at

23

The famous 'doctored' photo of a machine of 4.(St)/TrGr 186 returning from a raid on Hela with its undercarriage legs 'sheared off' after accidentally hitting the water . . .

. . . and the original shot used to create the fake, which in fact portrays a brace of *'Bertas'* of the *Condor Legion* over Spain!

sea. In the event, he managed to stagger back to base where he carried out a successful belly landing. The German propaganda machine seized upon this incident to extol the strength and structural integrity of the Stuka, claiming the undercarriage had been wiped off when the machine accidentally hit the water while pulling out of a dive. They even distributed a photograph purportedly showing the stricken machine during its return flight. The photo was a complete fake.

Having helped disable - or, to a greater or lesser extent, neutralise - Poland's air and sea forces in the opening hours of the invasion, the *Stukagruppen* were now freed to embark upon their main tactical role of 'flying artillery', clearing a path ahead, and to the flanks, of the advancing German Panzers and ground columns. The lightning war tactics of co-ordinated fire, support and rapid advance – the 'Blitzkrieg' – was about to be unleashed upon an unsuspecting Europe still immured in World War 1 traditions and practices.

Major Oskar Dinort, *Gruppenkommandeur* of I./StG 2 'Immelmann' recalls one of the earliest of such actions shortly after midday on 1 September when air reconnaissance brought back reports of large concentrations of Polish cavalry advancing on Wielun and threatening the northern flank of the German XVI.*Armeekorps.* After a short briefing by Oberstleutnant Baier in the bare wooden operations hut at Nieder-Ellguth (just completed, and still smelling strongly of freshly-sawn timber), Dinort and his three *Staffelkaitäne* hurried out to their aircraft;

'The engines spring into life. A wave to the groundcrew: chocks away! The *Stabskette* bumps across the uneven surface of the field, gathers speed and lifts off. A wide circle of the field to allow the following *Staffeln* to close up into formation . . . 30 steel birds on their first war flight!

'We cross the border at a height of 2500 metres. Visibility is far from good; hardly a kilometre. Although the sun is now shining, everything is swimming in an opalescent haze. Suddenly a group of buildings – either a large estate or a small village. Smoke is already rising. Wielun – the target!

'I stuff my map away, set the sights, close the radiator flaps; do all

Once the fog had lifted the *Stukagruppen* were on constant call to assist the advancing ground troops. Here, a unit waits in the September sun for its next mission, bombs having already been placed on the ground in readiness below the wings of the nearest aircraft – the risk of retaliatory strikes by the Polish Air Force was obviously not regarded as being very great!

Each machine carrying a single 500-kg bomb, a *Kette* lifts off from a forward field en route to a Polish target

Ju 87Bs echeloned to starboard, ready to peel off into a line-astern attack

25

Once over the target area each aircraft selected, or was assigned, a specific objective. This well-known photograph of a *'Berta'* unleashing a full load of single 250-kg bomb, plus four underwing 50-kg bombs, was also the subject of some propaganda skullduggery . . .

. . . for when placed against a different cloud formation, with an industrial landscape added below, another 'enemy' target can be shown to be facing certain destruction!

those things we've already done a hundred times or more in practice, but never with a feeling so intense as today. Then bank slightly, drop the left wing and commence the dive. The air brakes screech, all the blood in my body is forced downwards. 1200 metres – press the bomb release. A tremor runs through the machine. The first bomb is on its way.

'Recover – bank – corkscrew – and then a quick glance below. Bang on target, a direct hit on the road. The black snake of men and horses that had been crawling along it has come to a complete standstill. Now for that large estate, packed with men and wagons. Our height scarcely 1200 metres, we dive to 800. Bombs away! The whole lot goes up in smoke and flames.'

In mid-afternoon it was the turn of StG 77. For some of this unit's pilots it was already their fourth mission of the day (the first, scheduled at 04.45 hours, had been flown against Polish border fortifications near Lublinitz). The *Gruppe* logbook recorded, 'In complete contrast to the early morning, when we had quite literally taken off blind into the mist, the field was now bathed in sunshine. Not a cloud in the clear blue sky'.

All 60 Ju 87s of I. and II./StG 77 were ordered to concentrate their attack on the same large farm complex north of Wielun which, it had now

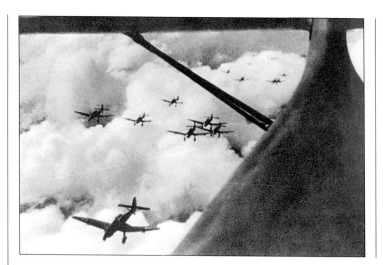

A daunting sight as serried ranks of
Ju 87s wing towards their objective

Poland's rail network suffered
heavily at the hands of the Stukas
as the Luftwaffe sought to disrupt
the enemy's lines of communication
and supply. Targets included
armoured trains, this one having
been derailed by a near miss on the
neighbouring track

been confirmed, housed the headquarters of the Polish *Wolynska* cavalry brigade. It was annihilated, the
troops scattered, and Wielun was
occupied by the advancing Germans that same night.

Thus, on the very first afternoon
of hostilities, the pattern had been
set for the remainder of the brief
campaign as Stukas and Panzers
combined to smash through
Poland's frontier defences (at the
same time, incidentally, providing
the world with an enduring image
of Polish cavalry gallantly charging
enemy tanks). For as the 24 infantry
divisions and six mounted brigades
of Poland's western armies were
pushed inexorably back – the
majority of them retiring towards
the capital, Warsaw – the Ju 87s
kept up their continual harassment.

No sooner did one of the 350+
reconnaissance machines (which
played such a vital role in the
Wehrmacht's success in Poland)
radio back a report, than a formation of Stukas would immediately
be despatched to the trouble spot,
be it a particularly stubborn defence position, a large body of enemy
troops, a road or rail line or a bridge offering a route of escape for the
retreating Poles.

As the German spearheads bit into Poland, so the close-support *Stukagruppen* had to move forward too in order to keep pace with them. Sometimes they ran the risk of overreaching themselves. Oskar Dinort again;

'We moved up into Poland. Our new base was some seven kilometres outside the town of Tschenstochau (Czestochowa). We arrived about midday and the base personnel immediately set about erecting tents and organising defensive positions. We were, after all, on enemy soil and the woods bordering the field to the north-east were reportedly full of Polish stragglers . . .

'. . . sure enough, hardly had darkness fallen before shots rang out from the edge of the woods. Our ground-staff replied with machine-guns and light flak. The whole field was eerily illuminated by flickering searchlight beams and red beads of tracer. The firing continued throughout the night, but died out shortly after 4 am when it started to rain. At last we air-crew could snatch some sleep.'

Dinort and his crews got all the rest they needed. The rain persisted, and they did not take off until 3 pm the next afternoon. Their targets were the bridges over the Vistula near the fort of Modlin, to the north of War-saw;

'We climbed through the grey clouds and broke out into clearer air at some 1200 metres. Below us the ragged valleys of cumuli, above us a leaden, sunless sky.

'Course north-east. Visibility was still not good. The windscreen streaked with more rain. Only the occasional glimpse of the ground and brief sighting of the Vistula through a break in the clouds to keep us on track. At last I saw the fort below us. It lay in the brown landscape, huge, grey and pointed like some burned-out star. And there too the Vistula bridges. Tiny lighter strips against the dark bed of the river: our target.

'The moment has come. Wing over into the dive! The machine drops like a stone. The altitude unwinds – down 200 metres, 300, 500. The

Bomb-laden *'Bertas'* press on to their target through thick banks of cloud

instruments can hardly keep pace with the rate of descent. Then the red veil in front of the eyes that every Stuka pilots knows. 1400 metres from the ground. . . 1200 metres . . . press the release. The bomb falls away into the depths below.

'I recover and take the usual evasive measures. Jinking away, I look back. Behind me the *Stabskette* are in the middle of their dive, the first *Staffel* right on their tails, dark shadows against the lightening sky. Their aim is good . . . one bomb hits the centre of the target.'

As the Polish retreat gathered pace and increasing numbers of their army units became compressed into ever smaller areas, dangerous pockets of potential resistance were created. South of Radom some six Polish divisions became thus entrapped while pulling back towards the safety of the Vistula. The encircling Panzers called up the Stukas to force them into surrender, Oberst Günter Schwartzkopff's I. and II./StG 77, reinforced by III./StG 51 and I./StG 76 (over 150 aircraft in all), pounding the hapless Poles. After enduring four days of near-constant attack, the banshee wail of diving Stukas dropping their deadly 50-kg fragmentation bombs and then ground-strafing with machine-guns, the demoralised survivors gave up.

An even greater danger threatened some days later. Completely surrounded west of Warsaw, the Polish *Poznan* Army – still practically intact – struck south-eastwards across the River Bzura, also aiming to reach the Vistula. This attempt to break through the thin screen of the German 8.*Armee* on the far bank of the Bzura would, if successful, completely cut off the forward most 10.*Armee*, which was already probing into the suburbs of Warsaw. *Heeresgruppe Süd* (Army Group South) sent out urgent appeals to the Luftwaffe for a 'maximum effort' against the Kutno area

Dropped from a I./StG 77 machine, this bomb narrowly missed a wide thoroughfare on the outskirts of Warsaw as Stukas supported the ground troops' advance on the Polish capital

A pair of Ju 87B-1s of Major Dinort's I./StG 2 'Immelmann', each armed with a single SC 250 (250-kg general-purpose) bomb, set out on another mission

As the *Blitzkrieg* drew to a close, formations of Stukas roared unchallenged and unopposed low over the flat plains of central Poland

(the centre of the 80-km wide Polish pocket).

In the ensuing 'Battle of Bzura Cauldron' – an essentially air-versus-ground engagement which finally broke the back of organised Polish resistance – the Stukas played a major role. Among them was I./StG 2;

'Take-off from our new base at Radom, an ex-Polish field, at 06.30 hours. A bright, clear autumn morning. We first steer a course north north-west to the confluence of the Vistula and the Bzura and then turn to follow the latter down to the target area . . .

'. . . a faint crackling in the earphones, like silk being torn. A report from the recce aircraft flying ahead of us; '"Achtung – Achtung! Falcon from Dove - Falcon from Dove. Strong enemy columns between III and I, and between II and IV – large concentrations at V and I. *Ende*".

'"Roger – Roger . . ." I reply. Before the start we had taken the precaution of "squaring up" a map of the target zone and numbering the salient points in case the enemy was listening in.

'I assign objectives to the individual *Staffeln* strung out behind me. Near Ilow we get our first sight of the enemy. A mass of artillery. Endless columns of troops and vehicles streaming eastwards in a broad flood, not just along the roads but also across the adjoining fields like a turgid grey river that has broken its banks.

'Wingover – dive – release bombs. Recover – climb – wingover – dive. Its hardly necessary to take aim. Such a target is impossible to miss. Then down to 200 metres and let fly with the machine-guns.

'We make our way singly back to base. fresh orders: "Refuel and rearm. *Gruppe* attack in area west of the Bzura".

'We land back from this second mission at 11.35 hours. A hurried meal of cold tinned meat and rice and then take-off for a third mission to the

Another mission successfully completed. If his gestures are anything to go by, the crewman on the left has all the makings of a top-scoring fighter ace!

Vistula-Bzura triangle, and a fourth . . .'

And so it went on until the last surviving remnants of the *Poznan* Army laid down their arms. With the danger to its rear eliminated, the *Wehrmacht* prepared for the final assault on Warsaw. The Luftwaffe, too, resumed its interrupted bombing campaign against the Polish capital. Initially, the *Stukagruppen* had been employed against specific pinpoint targets. These were often strongly defended and inevitably led to damage and losses among the attackers. Major Oskar Dinort describes an early raid on Warsaw;

Poland's rivers were a great aid to navigation in an otherwise often featureless landscape. A loosely-formated *Kette* overflies one such waterway, clearly delineated by the evening sun, as it makes its way back to base

'Today our target is the capital's radio station. We have orders to silence it by destroying the two large transmitter masts. We climb slowly up to 6000 metres. The air up here is thin and icy. At 4000 metres we had to put on our oxygen masks. But its ideal Stuka weather; scattered clouds to provide protection against enemy attack in an otherwise clear blue sky. The landscape below is bathed in sunlight and clear in every detail. We can follow our course as easily as if reading a map: there the bend of the Vistula at Auschwitz (Oswiecim, then simply another Polish community of some 10,000 souls, with none of the opprobrium which its German name now provokes), the railways thin bright ribbons, the roads dark against the pale yellow of the fields.

'Fifteen kilometres from the objective we begin a steep glide, engines throttled back to confuse the enemy's listening posts. 5000 metres . . . 4000 metres. The target comes into sight. One last check of the wind direction and then push the nose straight down.

'Ten seconds of vertical dive. You can't imagine how long those ten seconds can seem! Then press the button and a slight jolt as the 500-kg bomb leaves its cradle and plunges earthwards. Immediately recover and climb back up into the eye of the sun.

Oberleutnant Hartmann, *Staffelkapitän* of 3./StG 77, returned from a 6 September raid on Warsaw with the port wingtip and outer aileron of his 'Anton-Ludwig' in need of urgent repair!

Every extra second spent over the target is a gift to the enemy.

'A quick glance back. Always the same picture – seen dozens of times before but still as exciting as ever – the serried *Staffeln* in their dive, surrounded by bursts of flak; black this time, for the enemy is using his heavy artillery. The *Staffeln* reform for the return flight. Suddenly an ear-shattering racket in the cockpit. My observer has opened fire. Five Polish fighters have crept up on the first *Staffel* from behind and below. Their leader is less than 500 metres away.'

Generalfeldmarschall Hermann Göring, Luftwaffe C-in-C, visits I./StG 77 at their Radom base on 13 September. Among the high-ranking officers in attendance may be seen Generalmajor Wolfram *Freiherr* von Richthofen (OC of *Fliegerführer* z.b.V.), General Erhard Milch (Luftwaffe Inspector General) and Generalmajor Hans Jeschonnek (Chief of the Luftwaffe General Staff)

By the end of the campaign III./StG 2 'Immelmann' had been transferred south from Stolp, in Pommerania, to Vienne, in Slovakia. Here, at the foot of the High Tatra mountains, their purpose was to prevent the escape southwards of the last remnants of the Polish army. 8.*Staffel* unloads stores and provisions brought in by Ju 52 transports

The engine of this 8.*Staffel* machine gets a test run after having had some minor combat damage repaired

Hauptmann Hubertus Hitschhold's 1./StG 2 escaped unscathed on this occasion, but a 3. *Staffel* machine was not so fortunate – damaged by another group of enemy fighters, it crashed en route back to base killing both occupants.   Another, unnamed, Stabsfeldwebel attacking one of the Warsaw bridges on a later occasion also had good cause to remember the capital's anti-aircraft defences;

'I had just recovered from the dive and was corkscrewing back up to altitude when the Polish 40 mm flak caught me fair and square in its crossfire. The "red tomatoes" which this dangerous weapon spewed out were flying around my ears. Suddenly there was an almighty crash in the machine. There I was, 1200 metres over the middle of Warsaw, and I could tell immediately that the machine was no longer manoeuvrable.

'My gunner reported that the elevator had been shot off and there were only a few scraps left fluttering in the wind. Quick decision: the airfield just south of Warsaw was already in German hands. I had to make it. The machine was steadily losing height, but I slowly coaxed it along, gently sideslipped and got safely down at the first attempt.'

Damage to the Stukas such as this, and worse – rear fuselages split open, control surfaces shot away, one with its entire vertical tail missing save for a jagged stump of fin – are a much more valid, if lesser-known, testimony to the Ju 87's ruggedness than that famous 4.(St)/TrGr 186 Ju 87C-0 fake photo!

Despite inflicting much damage on Luftwaffe aircraft during the numerous raids on Warsaw, the city's anti-aircraft defences were eventually overwhelmed. By this stage most of the twin-engined bomber units had already been withdrawn to the west, leaving the final raids on the bat-

While the 8./StG 2 groundcrew, their work done, choose either to relax in the sun or seek the shade of a Stuka's wing, it is the SC 250 bomb in the foreground which here provides a wealth of detail for the modeller. Lying on its side, with its top towards the cameraman, it proves to be a two-fuse model, the two metallic fuse heads being clearly visible. The left-hand stencil ('15' in a circle) indicates a Type 15 electrical impact fuse, the middle stencil 'B' identifies the particular version of the bomb (one of eight), and the '14' refers to the type of explosive contained in the warhead. Note too the suspension eye bolt on the steel band and the lug seen here projecting upwards. The latter was one of two positioned on either side of the bomb and designed to engage the fork mechanism of the ventral cradle which swung the bomb clear of the propeller when it was released in the dive. The whole was normally finished in green-grey paint.

tered capital to be performed by Stukas dropping high-explosive bombs in level flight, followed by lumbering three-engined Ju 52s whose crews shovelled out incendiaries just to add to the carnage on the ground.

After Warsaw fell on 27 September there remained only the Modlin forts, some 25 kilometres to the north-west of the capital, to be subjugated. For the last time in Poland the Stukas gathered – units such as IV.(St)/LG 1, which had been exclusively briefed to pound the Baltic coastal defences, were brought in to add their weight to the attack. The Modlin defenders suffered several days of aerial onslaught before eventually surrendering to troops from the SS Regiment *Deutschland* on 29 September.

Forty-eight hours later Hela hoisted the white flag and it was all over. Poland had been overrun and a new word – *'Blitzkrieg'* – had entered the world's vocabulary. It had all cost the *Stukawaffe* just 31 Ju 87s.

NORWAY

By comparison, the *Wehrmacht's* next offensive venture could not be classed as *Blitzkrieg* in the accepted sense. The Norwegian campaign was strategic both in concept and execution. Firstly, it was mounted not only to safeguard Germany's supply of Swedish iron ore, which came by way of Norwegian waters, but also to quell Hitler's fears of a possible Allied invasion against his open northern flank. And secondly, Norway's mountainous terrain all but ruled out close Panzer/Stuka co-operation. The Germans did, however, spring some surprises with their extensive use of airborne transport, paratroops and ski-equipped mountain troops.

The only *Stukagruppe* to participate in the campaign against Norway was I./StG 1. After Bruno Dilley's opening raid of the war on Dirschau, this *Gruppe* had advanced into Poland acting as 'flying artillery' for the northern armies until its withdrawal back to East Prussia on 29 September.

By early 1940 it had been transferred to the west (Koblenz-Karthause to be exact), and was duly re-equipped with the Ju 87R. This was an extended-range version of the Ju 87B ('R' officially indicating *Reichweite*, or range), with additional auxiliary fuel tanks within the outer wing panels, and distinguishable externally by the two underwing drop tanks which replaced the *'Berta's'* normal 50-kg underwing bomb racks. Although thus restricted to a single, maximum 500-kg centre-line bombload, the *'Richard's'* range was almost doubled. In Norway, whilst the former would prove generally sufficient, the latter was essential.

While the bulk of the Luftwaffe units taking part in Operation *Weserübung* (*Weser Exercise*) began lifting off from their north German bases at dawn on 9 April 1940, Hauptmann Paul-Werner Hozzel's *Stukagruppe* sat out much of the opening morning of the invasion at Kiel-Holtenau. It was not until 10.59 hours that they were ordered to take-off. Their target was the fortress of Oscarsborg in Oslo

'A5+IH', a Ju 87R of 1./StG 1, shares a wintry Trondheim/Vaernes dispersal with a well wrapped up Heinkel He 111, probably of KG 26. Note the Stuka's underwing fuel tanks

Another 1.*Staffel* machine – 'Berta-Heinrich' – causes a minor snow storm as it taxis forward to the runway. Just visible on the engine cowling is I./StG 1's *Gruppe* badge, a diving raven, and a name – unfortunately indecipherable – which could well be commemorating a fallen comrade

Fjord, which had already been instrumental in sinking the 10,000-ton German cruiser *Blücher* with heavy loss of life. The attack by Hozzel's 22 Ju 87Rs had little effect on this occasion, however, and Oscarsborg did not surrender until after Oslo itself had fallen.

Having returned to their temporary forward field at Aarhus in Denmark, I./StG 1 were aloft again that same afternoon, heading not across the 250 kilometres of the Skagerrak back to Oslo, but this time out over the open sea in search of elements of the Royal Navy's Home Fleet, reported approaching the western coast of Norway. As the British ships were still too far off, Hozzel was instructed to turn back and land in Norway. The *Gruppe* altered course for the airfield at Stavanger-Sola, which had been captured during the morning. Just offshore they chanced upon a Norwegian destroyer, which they claimed to have attacked and sunk – their target had, in fact, been the 600-ton torpedo boat *Aeger*. Hit in the engine room, she was run aground and scuttled by her captain. I./StG 1's record of ship identification in the weeks ahead was to prove questionable to say the least!

While 2. and 3. *Staffeln* remained at Stavanger, 1./StG 1 was transferred to Trondheim, another of the ports simultaneously occupied by the Germans in the first hours of *'Weserübung'*. Initially operating from the surface of a frozen lake at Jonsvatnet, not far from the main Trondheim/Vaernes airfield, it was from here that the *Staffel* suffered its first combat loss when one of a *Kette* attacking British naval units in Namsenfjord on 19 April was damaged by anti-aircraft fire from HM cruiser *Cairo* – Leutnant Karl Pfeil and Obergefreiter Gerhard Winkels force-landed near Namsos and were taken prisoner. Six days later a raid on Trondheim/Vaernes by Skua and Swordfish aircraft from the carriers *Ark Royal* and *Glorious* cost 1./StG 1 six machines destroyed on the ground.

The *'Richards'* soon began hitting back, however. Before the month was out they had already sunk three Royal Navy anti-submarine trawlers – *Siretoco*, *Jardine* and *Warwickshire* – and badly damaged the sloop *Bittern* (which was later sunk by the destroyer HMS *Juno* when it became obvious she could not be repaired) all inshore in the Trondheim area.

HM sloop *Bittern* drifts helplessly after her stern was blown off by a Stuka's bomb at Namsos on 30 April 1940. Fires later spread throughout the vessel and she finally had to be sunk by a torpedo from the destroyer *Juno*

But it was on 1 May that I./StG 1 joined the major league when three separate waves of Stukas, guided by Heinkel He 115 floatplanes, were despatched several hundred kilometres out to sea to engage a Home Fleet formation which included both the aircraft carriers that had sent aircraft to Trondheim/Vaernes five days earlier. In the course of the ensuing attacks one 500-kg bomb narrowly missed *Ark Royal* by just a

Photographed from what appears to be the rear gunner's position of a low-flying Heinkel He 59 floatplane, a Ju 87R of I./StG 1 crosses Norway's coastline and heads out over the North Sea

matter of feet. It caused no serious damage, but this was not how Oberleutnant Heinz Böhme, *Staffelkapitän* of 2./StG 1, saw it;

'It was already late afternoon when we received report of the sighting. We took off in two *Ketten* and set course. We soon left the last rocky outcrops of the coastline behind us and headed out over open water . . . we had been flying over the ocean for almost an hour now, a somewhat risky business in a single-engined machine. The slightest hiccup and you could find yourself alone in the "drink", hundreds of kilometres from the nearest land. But our engines continued to behave perfectly.

'We sighted the enemy ships while still many kilometres away. With their long white wakes they looked like so many toys. But rather dangerous toys! As we drew nearer the flak rose to greet us. And now enemy fighters are on our tails too. We must attack immediately if we are not to waste our bombs. I select one carrier and order the other *Kette* to aim for the second. The flak is even thicker now as we start to dive.

'My target, the first carrier, seems to leap up at me at a fantastic rate, getting bigger and bigger. In a matter of seconds I have dived thousands of metres with my machine. I release the bomb and while recovering watch it strike dead centre in the forward third of the carrier's deck. But that's all I'm able to see. Like the rest of my comrades I'm at low level in the middle of the enemy ships and have to concentrate on getting clear.'

Böhme was convinced he had hit the *Glorious*, and fails to mention that one of his six Stukas (crewed by Oberfeldwebel Erich Stahl and Unteroffizier Friedrich Gott) was brought down by two defending Sea Gladiators that comprised 'Blue Section', No 802 Sqn. This proved to be I./StG 1's only loss in a hectic day of operations.

Scrambled from *Glorious* at 1800 hours, Lt J F Marmont and his wingman had initially been chasing a shadowing He 115C (of 2./KüFlGr 506 – it escaped before it could be engaged) when they saw three No 804 Sqn Sea Gladiators in the throes of attacking a V-formation of six Stukas, and decided to join in. Each fighter latched onto the tail of a Ju 87 and stayed with their respective targets until the latter rolled into their dives, but only Marmont could claim any success. Stahl managed to fly his mortally damaged Stuka some way back to Namsos, but eventually had to belly land the stricken dive-bomber some distance short of land – both he and Gott were quickly rescued by a British destroyer.

Having achieved little tangible results on the 1st, I./StG 1 made up for it some 48 hours later, as an anonymous gunner in one of the 14 Stukas, led by *Gruppenkommandeur* Hauptmann Paul-Werner Hozzel himself, graphically explains;

'Maritime reconnaissance (He 115Cs of 2./KüFlGr 506 again – Ed.) has reported a large English convoy retiring westward at full speed from the coast. The chase takes almost an hour and then the *Kommandeur's* voice in our earphones: "*Achtung!* To all aircraft. Prepare to attack!"

'Now we can see them, still far ahead, spread out and zig-zagging. Nerves begin to tighten as we approach. The ships become clearer and we can make out the differences between the merchantmen and the warships. Among the latter we spot some real heavyweights.

'We fly through black and white bursts of flak. The enemy is shooting at us with everything he's got. In the centre, heavy cruisers; unmistakable in size and with those superstructures. Further ahead the smaller destroyers. And there, a battleship! Much larger than all the others, ploughing through the water.

'We fly a wide circle around the convoy. The *Kommandeur* is obviously looking for the best angle of attack. All at once he stands his machine on its nose. That's the signal we've all been waiting for . . . as I watch the battleship a bomb strikes it squarely on the fo'c's'le. There is an eruption of blackish-grey smoke. Then a tremendous explosion. The magazine has probably been hit. A huge flame shoots skywards, another detonation, and now a gigantic column of fire and smoke towers over the battleship.'

Far from being a 'battleship', the Stukas' target was, in fact, the French super-destroyer *Bison* of 2436 tons. Her forward magazine had indeed received a direct hit, killing 108 members of her crew. After the survivors had been taken off, the stricken vessel was sunk by HMS *Afridi*, who was herself sent to the bottom, with the loss of 63 lives, by another wave of four Stukas shortly afterwards.

The next day elements of I./StG 1 scoured the fjords in the Namsos area again and sunk four Norwegian steamers (*Blaafjeld, Sekstant, Pan* and *Aafjorld*). On 8 May *Gruppenkommandeur* Hauptmann Hozzel, together with two of his pilots, Oberleutnant Elmar Schäfer (whose bomb had crippled HMS *Bittern*) and Leutnant Martin Möbus, plus veteran observer Unteroffizier Gerhard Grenzel, became the first four members of the *Stukawaffe* to be awarded the Knight's Cross (Grenzel being the first NCO of the entire Luftwaffe to be so honoured).

Melting Norwegian snow frames 1.*Staffel*'s 'A5+HH' as the campaign in Scandinavia draws to a close. Once again the *Gruppe* badge may just be made out on the cowling.

With the fight for central Norway at an end, attention turned to the Allies' one remaining foothold in the country around the iron-ore port of Narvik in the far north. Moving up to Mosjöen, I./StG 1 sank the armed Norwegian trawler *Ingrid* in Bodo harbour on 24 May and attacked the town's wireless masts and airstrip three days later. The latter mission resulted in the loss of a single Ju 87, flown by Feldwebel Kurt Zube, which was shot down by a Gladiator II of No 263 Sqn – one of three detached to Bodo to protect retreating British troops in the area. Flying the Gloster fighter was Flt Lt Caesar Hull, a battle-seasoned Rhodesian pilot who had joined the RAF in 1935. He had seen much action in the first months of the war at the controls of a No 43 Sqn Hurricane I off the coast of eastern Scotland, and had been posted to No 263 Sqn as a flight commander just prior to the unit's second deployment to Norway.

In the two days leading up to his Stuka kill, Hull had shot down or damaged three He 111s and a similar number of Ju 52/3ms in a hectic series of aerial engagements. On the 27th, he had been caught on the ground by the 11 marauding Ju 87s, and their trio of I./ZG 76 Bf 110C escorts. Having sat out the initial attack, Hull jumped in his Gladiator II during a brief lull in the bombing and strafing, and with the help of his fitter, managed to get the biplane started. He quickly took off and set chase after the trailing Stuka – Feldwebel Zube's Ju 87R. The latter was just levelling out at the bottom of its dive, and presented Hull with an easy target. He quickly shot it down into the sea, and its crew were soon retrieved by German troops.

The hunter now became the hunted, however, as Hull was firstly shot up by a second Stuka and then set upon by a Bf 110C flown by Leutnant Helmut Lent (who would score 113 kills – 105 by night – and win the Knight's Cross with Swords, Diamonds and Oakleaves, before being killed on 7 October 1944). The RAF pilot somehow managed to get back to his airfield in the crippled Gladiator II by flying at near tree-top height, but just as he was about to land, Lent hit the ailing biplane hard with an accurate burst of cannon fire and it crashed at Bodohalvoya – its pilot was wounded in the head and knee during the forced landing. Evacuated back to Britain soon afterwards, Hull recovered from his wounds and was posted back to No 43 Sqn as its CO on 31 August – whilst convalescing, he was awarded the DFC for destroying five aircraft in Norway. Sadly, Sqn Ldr Caesar Hull, DFC, was killed a week later during a dogfight with Bf 109s over South London.

Returning to Norway, on 2 June the Luftwaffe launched a final series of raids on Narvik itself. Three aircraft were lost by I./StG 1 on this day, two in the second wave to attack the port – Lt Klaus Küber and his gunner were killed when their Stuka crashed near Fagernes following an attack by a No 46 Sqn Hurricane I flown by Sgt B L Taylor, whilst Feldwebel Hans Ott and Sönderfuhrer Brack (the later attached to I./StG 1 as a war correspondent) survived with injuries after they were downed by Flg Off John F Drummond, who was also flying a Hurricane I from the same unit.

Drummond was the most successful Hurricane pilot to see action in Norway, downing four aircraft during his brief spell in Scandinavia. He later returned to England, where he was awarded the DFC and posted to No 92 Sqn on Spitfire Is. He had added a further four kills, plus numerous probables, to his score when he was killed in a collision with fellow No 92 Sqn ace Plt Off D G Williams on 10 October 1940 whilst attempting to shoot down a Do 17 over Brighton – the latter pilot also lost his life (see Osprey volume *Aircraft of the Aces 12 – Spitfire Mk I/II Aces 1939-41* for further details).

The third Stuka lost went down in the final wave to attack Narvik, and was being flown by *Staffelkapitän* Heinz Böhme of *Glorious* fame – it was last seen heading into the mountains with its port underwing tank ablaze. He had been leading another Ju 87 over Narvik when they had been intercepted by a pair of No 263 Sqn Gladiator IIs flown by Flt Lt A T Williams and Sgt H H Kitchener. The biplane fighters made short work of the *Staffelkapitan*'s Ju 87, but the second Stuka escaped into cloud and returned to base to report Böhme's apparent demise. Williams (a Canadian pre-war pilot) also shared another five He 111s as destroyed or probably destroyed with Kitchener on this day, and was subsequently recognised as having achieved ace status – like so many other No 263 Sqn pilots that managed to escape Norway, he was killed when *Glorious* was sunk by German battlecruisers some six days later.

On the same 2 June night that I./StG 1 began to realise that Heinz Böhme was gone for good, some 1350 miles away to the south the last British soldier was evacuated from the beach at Dunkirk . . .

THE LOW COUNTRIES AND FRANCE

The months of uneasy calm which settled over the western front following the subjugation of Poland - the so-called 'Phoney War' - saw little significant action as both sides busied themselves in preparation, the Anglo-French by manning their defences whilst the Germans gathered their forces for the attack. For the Luftwaffe the winter of 1939-40 was a period of rapid expansion, the numbers of both *Jagd-* and *Kampfgruppen* increasing by more than 50 per cent between September 1939 and May 1940 (from 18 to 29 and from 30 to 46 respectively).

It was all the more surprising then, given their success in Poland, that not a single new *Stukagruppe* was created during this period. The only addition to their ranks came about by raising the single *Staffel* 4.(St)/TrGr 186 to full *Gruppe* status. Although this brought their num-

The winter of 1939-40 was a time of rest and recuperation in the Homeland for the *Stukagruppen*. Few had it quite as cushy as the men of III./StG 2, however, their base at Ollesheim, outside Düren, being situated right alongside the local suburban tramline – a service much in demand at the end of the day's work!

With the spring came renewed preparations. In this parade-ground line-up of Ju 87B-1s, the coloured spinner tips of the first three machines (clearly darker than the brilliant white of 1.*Staffel* beyond) could well be green, indicating that they are the aircraft of the *Stabskette*

I.(St)/TrGr 186 utilised the winter months of 1939-40 to practise formation flying in their new-found *Gruppe* strength and, if this shot is anything to judge by, soon reached a high state of proficiency

bers to ten, I./StG 1's continued absence in Norway meant that the Luftwaffe embarked upon the campaign in the west marginally weaker in Stukas – in terms of both component *Staffeln* (down from 28 to 27) and serviceable machines – than when it had entered the war against Poland!

There had been a significant organisational change, however. Rather than dividing the Stukas evenly among the participating commands, as had been the case in Poland, two-thirds of their number were now concentrated in a single specialised corps (see the Appendices for details)

The planned assault in the west was divided into two distinct stages. Operation *Yellow* was to open with an all-out attack on Belgium and Holland, its aim being to draw the British and northern French armies out of their prepared positions along Belgium's western borders, and bring them forward to the aid of the two endangered neutral countries. Once the

A somewhat loosely tethered B-1 of StG 2 'Immelmann' awaits refuelling and arming. The fuel bowser on this occasion appears to be an impressed commercial vehicle, the name of its previous owner crudely overpainted and replaced by a Luftwaffe number plate. Note the different style of suspension attachment on this single-fuse bomb compared with that illustrated earlier

4./StG 77 armourers bombing up a Ju 87B-2. No white sidewall tyres on this trolley/hoist, the spit and polish of a peacetime régime having now given way to the realities of war . . .

Allies were out in the open and on the move north-eastwards, the major German thrust would be delivered to their rear, with armoured divisions sweeping around behind them and driving hard for the Channel coast. This would effectively isolate the northernmost Anglo-French forces in the Low Countries, which could then be defeated separately. Once this was accomplished the bulk of the *Wehrmacht* could launch the second phase of the campaign – Operation *Red* – the advance across the Somme, through the French heartland down to the Spanish and Swiss frontiers.

The spearheading VIII.*Fliegerkorps* would be heavily involved in all stages of this ambitious timetable. The months of March and April 1940 were therefore filled with a series of manoeuvres and dress rehearsals preparing the Stuka crews for the starring roles they were about to play. The key to the entire operation was the huge Belgian fort of Eben Emael. Built into the near-vertical sides of the Albert Canal (itself, in effect, an enormous 38-metre deep anti-tank ditch), the guns of the fort dominated the local countryside, including the Dutch border town of Maastricht and three vital bridges. These provided the axes for the 'feint' attack on Belgium. If Eben Emael could not be neutralised at once – essentially if its heavy guns remained intact to destroy the bridges – the whole edifice of the plan of campaign would crumble.

Even against such antiquated fortresses as Modlin and Oscarsborg the

. . . and no mechanical assistance at all for this trio of 'black men' as they struggle to lift a 50-kg bomb on to the port underwing ETC bomb-rack of another Ju 87

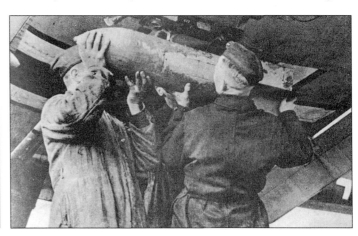

An armourer festooned with belts of 7.9 mm ammunition prepares to load the wing machine-guns of Stuka 'A-Anton' seen in the background

effect of Stuka bombardment had not been immediate. And Eben Emael was a far tougher proposition altogether. Completed only five years earlier, its three underground levels were topped by massive concrete casemates, heavily armoured dome-shaped steel cupolas and batteries of anti-aircraft guns. With an authorised strength of 1200 officers and men, Eben Emael was considered impregnable. Yet, as it transpired, the fortress was captured by just 78 airborne troops landing by glider on its grassy surface area at dawn on 10 May 1940 in a now historic *coup de main*. Armed with revolutionary hollow-shaped charges, they set about disabling the armoured gun emplacements. The door for Operation *Yellow* was open.

All is ready. The groundcrews can relax, the aircraft tarpaulined and camouflaged, as a group of officers (right) await further orders

Also aloft at first light that day, the Stukas had no less an important role to perform. While waves of Ju 87s of StG 2 pounded the peripheral defences of the fort and the nearby village of Eben Emael to prevent reinforcements from reaching its west-facing entrance tunnel, four of their number pin-pointed a building in the village of Lanaeken, some 14 kilometres along the Albert Canal to the north. This was the headquarters of the Belgian officer responsible for ordering the demolition of the three canal bridges should they appear to be in danger of falling into German hands. The weeks of practice which the four pilots had put in for this one attack paid off. The HQ was blasted into rubble before the *Commandant* could transmit the necessary orders.

Despite the subsequent confusion one bridge was blown up in the face of the advancing Germans. Troops poured across the other two. In the days ahead these structures would become the target for near-suicidal Allied bombing attacks and provide the setting for the RAF's first two VCs of World War 2.

While the now Major Dinort's StG 2 was thus engaged against the Albert Canal and its defences, StG 77, led by Oberst Günter Schwartzkopff, had taken off from Cologne-Butzweilerhof to attack other frontier fortifications along the River Meuse to the south around Liège. That evening the two *Geschwader* combined forces to mount a major dive-bombing raid on the port of Antwerp.

The opening day of the invasion had cost over a dozen Stukas, most of them from Dinort's *Gruppen* (including seven from the subordinate I./StG 76 alone) and all to anti-aircraft fire. Twenty-four hours later it was the turn of Allied fighters to inflict casualties among the ranks of the Ju 87s. And again it was StG 2 which bore the brunt.

The first air battle of the campaign in the west erupted just east of Brussels when some 60 Ju 87s of StG 2 were attacked by six RAF Hurricane Is of No 87 Sqn. It was in the ensuing melée between Tirlemont and St Trond that the Stuka's basic flaws – its deficiencies in speed, armour and defensive armament – were first brought home to the men flying it. Despite forming a defensive circle (a manoeuvre in itself a tacit admission of inferiority), they forfeited six of their number, plus another damaged. It was only the Allies' own growing confusion and disorganisation in the weeks of withdrawals and retreat to come that would save them from even heavier losses.

For the push across Belgium had already begun. Among the first units to move into occupied terri-

Signallers of an air landing unit wave greetings to one of the Stukas which provided them with such effective close support during their initial airborne assault on the Low Countries

43

A mechanic checks the glycol level of a Ju 87B-1. Groundcrews were able to witness at first hand the destructive power and pinpoint accuracy of their charges as Stukas battered Belgian defences in full view of their own forward landing grounds

tory were elements of StG 77. IV.(St)/LG 1 were ordered forward to Bierset, west of Liège, on only the second day of the fighting – it was a calculated risk which very nearly came to grief. The ground echelon had just begun to clear the field of debris from the opening day's bombing raids when they came under fire from the guns of Fort Flémalle, one of Liège's outer ring of fortifications.

Fortunately, the *Gruppenkommandeur* himself landed at Bierset during a lull in the bombardment. After being appraised of the situation, he took off to lead IV.(St)/LG 1 in an attack on the offending fort, just visible on the horizon. The action that followed moments later afforded the ground personnel a grandstand view of the destructive power wielded by an unopposed *Stukagruppe* in full cry. The fort gave them no more trouble, although it would not be until 17 May, and in the wake of a further attack by StG 2, that Flémalle finally surrendered, being one of the last of the Liège forts to do so. By that time the Germans had entered Brussels, but not without further losses to StG 2 on the way, as Oberleutnant Lothar Lau, Kapitän of 8. *Staffel*, recounts;

'We are briefed to attack road and rail targets between Tirlemont and Louvain. Unusually favourable weather; three-tenths cloud in an other-

One of the forts along the Meuse, possibly Flémalle itself, bears the scars of a concentrated Stuka attack while the surrounding orchards and countryside remain unscathed

Heavily camouflaged by branches
and shrubs, Ju 87 T6+LS of 8./StG 2
'Immelmann' is refuelled in the open
on a makeshift landing strip

wise perfectly blue May sky. I lead my two *Kettenhunde* (wingmen) towards Tirlemont. Let's see what's happening at the railway station. Nothing doing. We've been here once today already. Troops of all kinds are streaming into town from the east. Climb over the southern suburbs for a quick look at the airfield, but the nest is empty. So back to a large cross-roads on the eastern edge of town, dive gently without using the brakes and plant our bomb smack in the middle of the crossing. "The whole corner house has collapsed into the street!" reports my wireless-operator excitedly.

'Out over the rooftops followed by machine-gun fire. Suddenly a loud bang. Then two more in quick succession. I recognise that noise from Poland. We've been hit. It suddenly smells strongly of petrol. And there, in the wing, the jagged exit holes are clearly visible.

'The rest of the *Staffel* are still west of town, my two *Kettenhunde* several streets away. Another hit knocks out the radio. I give the visual signal to reform but everybody is too busy to notice. I circle, but my fuel is running out fast. So we set off alone, hedge-hopping eastwards at ground level.

'St Trond comes into sight, we pass it to the south. After a while the unmistakable silhouette of the cathedral at Tongres. Once past that and we're home and dry. The leading *Panzers* are already pushing south-westwards out of Tongres. Set course for Maastricht - maybe we can even make it as far as Aachen!

'Suddenly the voice of the wireless-operator in my earphones: "Enemy fighters, two Hurricanes!" My question, are they attacking us, is drowned out by the racket from the rear cockpit as he opens fire. Now at least I know! I try to use every dip in the ground and scrap of cover I can find. My wireless-operator calls out the direction of the attack each time the enemy closes in for the kill.

'I heave the machine to left and right, always turning into the side the attack is coming from, but all the while slowly gaining a little more ground eastwards. We take more hits. The two *Engländer* have me well and truly boxed in: if I turn towards one, the other lets fly at me with all he's got.

'Bullets fly past either side of me. More strikes in the fuselage. My wire-

45

less-operator is hit. In the mirror I can see him slumped over his gun. Again the machine shudders under a hail of fire – the elevators don't respond any more. Blood is flowing down the side of my face. The engine has been hit too – it's coughing badly and oil covers the windscreen.

'I shout to the wireless-operator: "Hang on. We're going down!" An automatic grab at the brakes and flaps. I use the rudder to try to steer the machine between the fruit trees directly ahead of us. We make it. I clamber out and pull the unconscious wireless-operator clear. The first ground troops are soon on the scene and an ambulance is quickly organised to take him to hospital in Maastricht. But my trusty old "Anton-Siegfried" is a sorry sight in the middle of the orchard, fuselage broken in two, half of one wing missing and the nose pointing up at the still, clear, blue sky.'

As soon as the northern Anglo-French forces were fully committed to their advance into central Belgium, the main blow fell. German armoured columns burst out of the 'impenetrable' Ardennes to the south and raced for the one obstacle in their path – the River Meuse at Sedan. Once that had been crossed the way to the Channel coast would be wide open.

The whole of VIII. *Fliegerkorps* was temporarily seconded to *Luftflotte* 3 for the attack on French positions guarding the Meuse crossings. On 13 May they struck. In just five hours that day StG 77 alone flew more than 200 individual sorties. Towards evening the weather closed in and flying was restricted, but by that stage the Stukas had done their job. The combined onslaught from the air and from the ground – the ear-splitting wail of engines and sirens from the diving Stukas overhead punctuating the constant rumble of Panzer and artillery fire from across the river – had completely demoralised the French defenders. Within 48 hours the Meuse had been successfully breached.

14 May over the Sedan bridgeheads has gone down in Luftwaffe history as the 'Day of the Fighters', the *Jagdwaffe's* Bf 109s annihilating the Allied bombers attempting to deny the crossings to the advancing Germans. The *Stukagruppen*, too, also suffered casualties along the Meuse on that date (11 aircraft fell to flak or Allied fighters), with no single loss being more keenly felt than that of Oberst Günter Schwartzkopff, *Kommodore* of StG 77, whose Ju 87 received a direct hit from French anti-aircraft fire over Le Chesne near Sedan.

Schwartzkopff's untiring efforts before the war in promoting the dive-bomber's cause had earned him the title of 'The father of the Stukas'. His dedicated service since, which had seen him at the head of StG 77 during every major action in Poland and the west to date, being recognised by posthumous promotion to Generalmajor and the award of the Knight's Cross.

On 18 May another, perhaps more familiar, name associated with the Stuka also received the Knight's Cross. Ironically, Generalmajor Wolfram *Freiherr* von Richthofen, World War 1 fighter pilot and cousin of the legendary 'Red Baron', had originally voiced strong opposition to the dive-bomber back in 1936 while serving as head of development of the *Technisches Amt* (Technical office) under the flamboyant Ernst Udet – the financing of those two Curtiss Hawks had done the trick! Nor was he overly enamoured of the Ju 87's performance in Spain three years later when C-in-C of the *Legion Condor*. Yet, it was this self-same machine

Wireless-operator's view of his pilot scanning the summer sky. Although not wearing goggles, he is looking into the sun – the likeliest direction of an enemy fighter attack

which, under von Richthofen's overall command, had paved the way for victory in Poland, and was even now carving a swathe through northern France.

For with the broad waters of the Meuse behind them, the five Panzer divisions of 12. *Armee*, supported by von Richthofen's VIII. *Fliegerkorps*, had their sights firmly set on the Channel coast. The armoured dash across France during that third week of May 1940 – the very epitome of *Blitzkrieg* – was perhaps the Stuka's 'finest hour'. Responding to the Panzers' every call, they cleared pockets of potential resistance ahead of the route of advance, broke up the penny-packet Allied tank attacks along its flanks, harried rear-area reinforcements – many of whom were filled with dread by the mere mention of the word 'Stuka' – and hampered much of the enemy's troop movements by the panic they spread along the refugee-filled roads.

In order to keep abreast of the advancing ground forces, the *Stuka-gruppen* were constantly moving forward too. They took up temporary residence on whatever suitable piece of ground presented itself, be it an abandoned enemy airfield or just a level patch of cow pasture. But the 'Bertas' often still found themselves operating at the very limit of their range, and the timely arrival of the first Ju 87Rs on the western front at this juncture provided a source of much needed, longer-legged, rein-forcement.

At the height of the advance, while brushing aside the remnants of French Gen Bruneau's 1st Armoured Division outside St Quentin, the *Blitzkrieg* steamrollered over the very area where Harry Brown's little S.E.5a had first dive-bombed in anger some 22 years earlier. On 18 May StG 2 twice attacked troop trains in Soissons station, whilst 24 hours later their bombs not only blocked the exits from Amiens but also broke up a counter-attack by French tanks outside Laon.

The Stukas move up into Belgium. A Ju 87B-1 of StG 2 'Immelmann' rests awhile at St Trond, flanked by the skeletal remains of a pair of Belgian Air Force Fiat C.R.42 biplane fighters

On 20 May spearheads of the 2.*Panzerdivision* reached the Channel. The British and Belgian armies, plus a large number of French troops, were now isolated within a large pocket with their backs against the sea around Dunkirk. While some *Stukagruppen* concentrated on reducing the perimeter of this pocket, preventing any attempts at breaking out southwards to rejoin the main body of French forces, others began to invest the Channel ports.

21 May thus witnessed elements of StGs 2 and 77 attacking troop concentrations between Arras and St Pol on the southern flank of the pocket, as one StG 77 pilot remembers only too well;

'The ring around Flanders has been closed. Enemy troops have been reported gathering near Arras, and that's where our nine machines are heading. I keep a close watch ahead and below: canals, sunken barges, destroyed bridges, roads, columns of troops, a forest – another canal – and then our target.

'"Prepare to attack!" A few final checks and we wing over into a steep dive. The edge of town, there's the large cross-roads – and masses of troops. I push old "Anton" ever steeper. Black-grey puffs of smoke suddenly surround me – then a dangerous spider's web of red tracer. 3000 metres, 2500, 2000 – the tightly-packed column dances in front of my eyes, unfocused, fuzzy, but growing larger by the second. A slight jolt as I release the bomb and climb away at full throttle.

'Then a bang – and the machine starts to shudder violently. The engine stutters and begins to smoke. I check the controls, trying this lever and that - hopeless . . .

'A voice in my earphone: "Anton from Dora, your machine is smoking badly!" For God's sake, as if I hadn't noticed that myself already! "Anton – attempting to reach the front south of Arras", I reply.

Snapshot of the great advance – a member of III./StG 2 'Immelmann' takes time off to do some laundry. A bush makes a handy washing line

'"Will we make it?" my gunner enquires quite calmly. "Yes, but there's a lot of fuel sloshing about up front here. If that goes up, get out immediately". Slowly, the whole machine vibrating and emitting clouds of smoke, we creep southwards. Surely we must reach Arras soon.

'Whoompf! With a sound like a gas boiler exploding, "Anton" is suddenly engulfed in flames. "That's it, Out!!"

'Undo the harness, release the canopy and jump as the machine noses into its last dive. The wind hits me. A tug and the 'chute opens above my head. As I emerge from a layer of cloud I see below me another parachute – my gunner! Thank God, he's made it too!'

On the Belgian (eastern) flank of the pocket other *Gruppen* were attacking the Armentières-Estaires-Bailleul triangle where enemy troops were so thick on the ground that veterans of the Polish campaign likened the scene below to that along the Bzura eight months earlier.

Meanwhile, the Channel ports were being rolled up one by one as the Panzers advanced northwards along the coast from the mouth of the Somme. Boulogne was occupied on 25 May after heavy raids by II./StG 2 and I.(St)/TrGr 186. The next day it was the turn of Calais,

A mix of dining-room chairs and deckchairs for this group of officers of 10.(St)/LG 1 relaxing over a game of chess. 'Cäsar-Ulrich' ('L1+CU') waits patiently in the background, but the pile of beer glasses on the table presumably indicates no more flying today!

There are far fewer comforts of home for the 'black men' – just a bomb for a card table and tool boxes to sit on. The aircrew Feldwebel on the right seems quite dejected by the injustice of it all

when the remnants of the Rifle Brigade, holed up in the town's Citadel, were forced to surrender after a 'horrific Stuka bombardment' by StGs 2 and 77.

With smoke from the burning port obscuring the town from the south, the Ju 87s had to attack from seaward. Crossing the coastline north-east of Calais, they flew out over the Channel conscious of England's chalk cliffs bathed in sunshine on their right ('so close you could almost touch them!'), and all too aware of the enemy's fighter bases just behind those cliffs.

Over the next few days, for the first time since the start of the campaign in the west, the *Stukagruppen* would again suffer heavily. But one unidentified pilot, obviously an ex-*Condor Legion* man, had a lucky escape;

'We were somewhere over Calais in our *Jolanthe* with orders to drop our "big one" on the Citadel. But that's no easy job when you've got three English fighters sitting on your tail. They had appeared out of nowhere from a cloud and had already turned my starboard wing into a sieve. "*Ei, Donnerwetter*", I thought, "three fighters, that makes 24 machine guns – and all shooting at me".

'Old *Jolanthe* had caught quite a packet. And to make matters worse my gunner had been wounded . . .'

He nevertheless managed to escape further damage and get away, only for his engine to give up. He began to glide inland;

'. . . after a few kilometres – we were quite low by then – I saw the recognition panels of a German infantry unit laid out in a large field. The machine landed heavily and immediately somersaulted over onto its back. That told yours truly something that hadn't been apparent before – the tyres had been shot to pieces too!

'My gunner and I were trapped underneath the machine in a somewhat

Already bombed-up, Ju 87B-2 'T6+HL' of 3./StG 2 'Immelmann' undergoes last-minute preparations for its next sortie

uncomfortable position and unable to move. But we soon heard sounds of spades and shovels and ten minutes later we were on our way, still a bit groggy, to the field hospital. The MO patched us up with all the usual sympathy of a frontline medic – "Some people are just too stupid to get themselves killed" – and next day we were in a transport Ju heading for hospital back in Germany.'

There now remained just the one prize to complete Operation *Yellow* – Dunkirk.

Although some rear echelon troops and other supernumeraries

With the crew now aboard and the thin screen of camouflage branches removed (but with the makeshift chocks still in place) 'Heinrich-Ludwig's' engine is cranked up. Note that the *Staffel* badge is carried on both sides of the fuselage below the windscreen, but that the aircraft's individual letter 'H' is repeated on the front of the starboard wheelspat only – incidentally, the yellow-tipped spinner on this machine appears to have taken a nasty knock!

had begun returning to England as early as 20 May, Operation *Dynamo* – the planned evacuation of the BEF – was not officially put into effect until the evening of 26 May. That same day Göring had ordered his Luftwaffe to make Dunkirk its priority target. The beginning of the evacuation in earnest thus coincided with an escalation of the previous days' air attacks. At dawn on 27 May two *Kampfgeschwader* mounted a raid on the town and port, and later in the day the *Stukagruppen* added their weight to the assault, one of their victims being a large French cross-Channel steamer.

The weather favoured the Allies for the next 36 hours, low cloud and rain over the target area and beyond greatly reduced the Luftwaffe's effectiveness. But by the afternoon of 29 May conditions had improved sufficiently to allow full-scale air operations to resume;

'The bad weather meant that we hadn't been able to "lay our morning eggs" – our description for the first sortie of the day – but now fresh orders had arrived by messenger. Target Dunkirk!

'Dark columns of smoke show us the way, although it still isn't ideal Stuka weather. Huge banks of clouds reaching down almost to ground level greatly hamper downward visibility. As we each try to keep in touch with the man in front through the scudding cloud and smoke from the burning town, red tramlines of tracer from the light flak combine with explosions from heavier calibre guns to create an almost impenetrable curtain.

'The machine in front of me tips slowly onto its nose and disappears into its dive. At that moment I spot a gap in the clouds and see beneath me a harbour wall, a large loading ramp and – I can hardly believe my eyes – a nice fat freighter tied up alongside. I run my hands over the controls almost by instinct. Now it's just stick forward, and the old crate stands on its head as down we go straight at the target.

'An absolute wall of flak comes up at me. Quickly, a few random bursts from my wing guns in reply. I align the machine onto the target, take careful aim through the sight and release my bomb. While recovering, I look back to check the result – where the ramp had been there is now a rising column of fire and smoke.'

This combined attack by three *Stukagruppen* had been concentrated on the Dunkirk mole, which was packed with ships busily embarking troops.

A direct hit scored by I./StG 77 on one of the 'little ships' taking part in the Dunkirk evacuation on 1 June 1940. Note the near misses of the Kettenhunde aft of the stricken vessel

The detritus of Dunkirk. Wrecked Austin vehicles of the BEF, immobilised and abandoned on the cratered and littered beach. The three-funnelled vessel in the background with its bow blown off is the 1278-ton French destroyer l'Adroit, sunk and stranded by air attack on 21 May

The destroyer HMS *Grenade* was sunk and others hit and badly damaged. Many smaller merchant vessels were also lost, including the Thames paddle-steamer *Crested Eagle*. As a result, no further major evacuation attempts were made from the mole, the bulk of the remaining troops being lifted straight off the beaches.

Another spell of bad weather kept the Stukas grounded for the last two days of May, but on 1 June they were back again with a vengeance. In a series of raids lasting all day (some crews flying as many as three or four sorties), they took a heavy toll of Allied shipping. One pilot managed to plant his bomb straight down the aft funnel of HMS *Keith*, one of three RN destroyers sunk off Dunkirk that day, whilst others went after the merchantmen, as this *Kettenführer* recounts;

'Back again to Dunkirk. A quick glance at the transport we caught this morning. A complete wreck, stern under water, listing badly. Again we've split up into separate *Ketten*, each looking for individual targets. But all the "choice items" close inshore have already been hit. We head a little further out to sea. There, a 2000-tonner making northwestwards at top speed. After him! I signal my two wingmen to close up on me. We're a bit low, but it'll have to do. I drop my second "ration" of the day - damn, a miss - but just wait, my friend, there are two more behind me . . .

'. . . for the third time today over Dunkirk. Still nothing but wrecks and floating wreckage off the beaches. But further out, some 20 km from the coast, an assortment of ships running for safety. The *Engländer* are using everything they've got to take their troops back across the Channel. Off the port quarter a tug towing a good-sized barge. A worthwhile target, but another *Kette* gets there before us.

'Suddenly a transport hoves into view, hidden until now under cloud. I point him out to my wingmen and down we go. My bomb hits the water immediately ahead of him. His bow slices into the white circle on the surface marking its passage . . . now his midships are directly above the point of entry . . . Crrump!! The middle of the ship is lifted out of the water –

Ju 87B-2s of I./StG 77 stand
camouflaged among the trees
bordering the field at Courcelles,
near St Quentin, ready for the
second phase of the campaign
against France

pieces fly 100 metres into the air. We watch him start to settle when suddenly, "Fighter left!" my gunner yells.

'The Spitfire curves in to attack from the rear. "Range 300 metres . . . 200 metres" . . . Franz intones in my earphones. I start to bank, "100 metres" . . . Franz looses off a burst of machine gun fire. The Tommy breaks right. He comes in again from that side – makes a third pass – and then disappears.

'We've got off lightly. Just a slight oil leak from a fractured pipe. "He was only shooting with his four starboard guns", Franz remarks as we head home . . . "Our lucky day then", I reply, "Otherwise we might have ended up in the drink in the middle of all those Tommies. Damned cheek, though, not letting us see what happened to our transport!"'

In fact, by the end of the day the Allied evacuation fleet had lost a total of 31 ships sunk, with 11 seriously damaged and many others having suffered savage strafing attacks. Late on 2 June the signal 'BEF evacuated' was made, although the formal French surrender of Dunkirk did not take place until the morning of 4 June. By then, however, VIII.*Fliegerkorps* had already wheeled about and was preparing to strike southwards across the Somme. Operation *Red* was about to begin.

This second phase of the *Wehrmacht*'s almost clinical invasion and defeat of metropolitan France was launched on 5 June. For von Richthofen's Stukas, the next fortnight degenerated into a series of dashes to, and across, one river line after the other as the French retreat gathered momentum. Initially tasked with supporting the armour of *Panzergruppe* von Kleist across the Somme between Amiens and Péronne, and with assisting 9.*Armee*'s breaking through the Weygand Line around Laon, VIII.*Fliegerkorps* was then to cover the spearheads of 2.*Armee* down to the Swiss border.

The first 72 hours saw the French thrown back across the Somme, the Oise and the Aisne as the Panzers raced for the next natural great water barrier, the River Marne, east of Paris. The *Stukagruppen* were in constant attendance, on call to strike at the first signs of any organised enemy resistance, and attacking bridges to disrupt the French lines of retreat. A German war correspondent gave a graphic account of one such sortie flown on 7 June;

'Yesterday, we were over one of the main assembly points for enemy troops – a town some ten minutes' flying time east of Paris, which was just visible through the layer of smoke and haze which covers every large city. Otherwise, the sky was as bright and cloudless as only a summer sky can be. We sat under the glass canopy of the cockpit as if in some flying greenhouse, suffering the full effect of the sun. You could feel the sweat trickling down your back under the one-piece flying overalls and beading your forehead below the tightly-fitting helmet. A few small specks in the distance were our fighter escort. Our *Kette* kept tight formation as we approached the target. Others flew to the left and right of us.

'"Fasten your harness, we're diving!" the pilot called out. It was almost as if – for a split second – the machine hung motionless in the sky. Then the tail rose almost vertically as the nose tipped earthwards. The flow of air built up, whistling over the wing surfaces and beating against the cabin windows. The ground – a moment ago a relief model unfolding below us with contours, hills and a horizon – was suddenly a flat map filling our entire field of vision . . . a map whose details were growing sharper and larger by the second!

'The pilot hung motionless in his seat, his right eye pressed against the sight as he concentrated on the target. The howl of the engine rose and drowned the noise of the wind. There's the bridge! His finger pressed the button on the control column marked with the word "Bombs". A slight jolt. On either side of us, swaying gently only some 30 metres away, the two *Kettenhunde* released their bombs in perfect unison.

'At almost the same moment I was pressed down hard in my seat as the pilot began to pull out. I swallowed to relieve the pressure in my ears. The wings flexed slightly. Then we were flying horizontally, but jinking to the left and right, rising and falling, to throw the enemy flak gunners off their aim as we reformed for the homeward flight. Three hours later aerial photographs showed the bridge to be completely destroyed.'

On 12 June the Germans crossed the Marne near Château-Thierry. The next day Paris was declared an open city. Despite the growing chaos and confusion of the French retreat, the *Stukagruppen* continued to encounter small pockets of individual resistance, both on the ground and in the air, as they swept southwards past France's undefended capital off to their right. I./StG 2 had already destroyed some 20 to 30 tanks gathering to launch a counter-attack on the Germans' unprotected flank to the north of the city. On 13 June a *Staffel* of StG 77, based south-east of Soissons, was ordered to attack the railway line between Troyes and Auxerre. They had just flown over the leading Panzers near Montmirail when;

'. . . something caught the *Staffelkapitän*'s attention; small dots in the distance far ahead. He watched the gaggle of tiny specks swooping and diving among the clouds. Must be our fighter escort, he thought. "They're in a good mood today!" he said to his wireless-operator.

'Off to the left enemy flak tried a few tentative ranging shots. Nothing to upset the *Staffel* there. They maintained course. The fighters approached in a wide right-hand curve. At least 30 of them . . . a whole *Gruppe*! Funny though, they've split up into three *Staffeln* and are still closing in. Oddest thing of all, they are flying in *Ketten* of threes just like us . . . but our fighters usually operate in *Schwärmen* of fours? The light suddenly dawns: they're French.

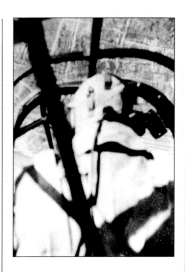

'. . . a flat map filling our entire field of vision. . .' Although taken during a simulated attack on a German town, this picture graphically offers a pilot's-eye view of the target during a near vertical dive

THE *BLITZKRIEG* ERA

'"Haven't seen so many Frenchmen since Sedan", the *Staffelkapitän* thinks to himself as the wireless-operator opens fire. The smell of cordite fills the cabin. The *Kapitän* waits until he sees the lines of tracer shooting past. Now! "Turn into them!" As one, his pilots – veterans all – bank towards the enemy fighters and open fire with their wing guns. It was a manoeuvre they had thoroughly practised all winter long back in Cologne – practised until they were heartily sick of it. But now it was paying dividends.'

Taken by surprise, the French fighters were forced to break to avoid the oncoming Stukas. As they flashed past each other the Stukas' rear gunners let fly, claiming at least two of the enemy which were seen going down trailing smoke. But it was the arrival of the Bf 109 escort which saved the Ju 87s from further attack (and almost certain losses), and which accounted for nine of the French Moranes.

Forty-eight hours later the whole of I./StG 77 was back over the Auxerre region bombing and strafing a stubborn nest of French troops holed up in a group of fortified buildings. On 16 June the Germans crossed the Seine. The next day, despite unseasonably bad weather, the Stukas were attacking enemy columns around Dijon and supporting bridgeheads over the River Loire near Nevers.

The end was now in sight. Marshal Pétain had appealed for an armistice on 17 June – that day too German reconnaissance aircraft reported no large enemy formations along the Loire or Saône rivers, or anywhere beyond right up to the Swiss border. On 18 June von Richthofen ordered two-thirds of VIII.*Fliegerkorps* to stand down, although signs of renewed French activity north of Dijon later in the day resulted in a last flurry of Stuka attacks, and the reported surrender of three French divisions soon afterwards.

Ironically, 18 June also witnessed the final Ju 87 losses of the entire campaign when two aircraft of III./StG 51 collided over Nivelles – the last of some 120 Stukas lost to all causes since 10 May.

By 19 June VIII.*Fliegerkorps* was being held at readiness on bases around the Nevers-Auxerre areas of central France. However, the mission scheduled for the following day was cancelled, the advance halted, and the ground forces withdrawn to the newly agreed demarcation line between occupied and unoccupied (Vichy) France. Forty-eight hours later the Armistice was signed at Compiègne.

And so the Stukas never made it to the Swiss border. Instead they were ordered to execute another 180° turn, for while much of the Luftwaffe retired to the Homeland for a well deserved and much needed rest and refit, von Richthofen's VIII.*Fliegerkorps* were to put their proven precision attack capabilities to another, more immediate, use. In the last weeks of June they headed back up to France's battle-scarred northern coast, their new task, to close the English Channel to British shipping.

Despite the success of the *Blitzkrieg* in western Europe, the Stukas had paid a price. In addition to some 120 aircraft lost or written-off during the campaign, many more were damaged. This machine of StG 2, sieved by bullet holes and shrapnel and minus its landing gear fairings and all other unnecessary weight, is setting off back to Germany for repair. The journey will have to be made in short hops, for every fuel tank except one has been shot to pieces!

55

COLOUR PLATES

This ten–page colour section profiles many of the aircraft flown in combat by the *Stukageschwader* between 1937 and 1941. All the artwork has been specially commissioned for this volume, and profile artist John Weal and figure artist Mike Chappell have gone to great pains to illustrate the aircraft, and their crews, as accurately as possible following in-depth research from original sources. Ju 87s that have never previously been seen in profile are featured alongside acccurate renditions of some of the more familiar Stukas of the period. The profiles appear in unit establishment order.

1
Ju 87B-1 '35+G12' of 2./StG 163 'Immelmann', Cottbus, February 1939

2
Ju 87A-1 '35+Y25' of 5./StG 163 'Immelmann', Grottkau/Silesia, January 1939

3
Ju 87A-1 '52+A12' of 2./StG 165, Pocking, March 1938

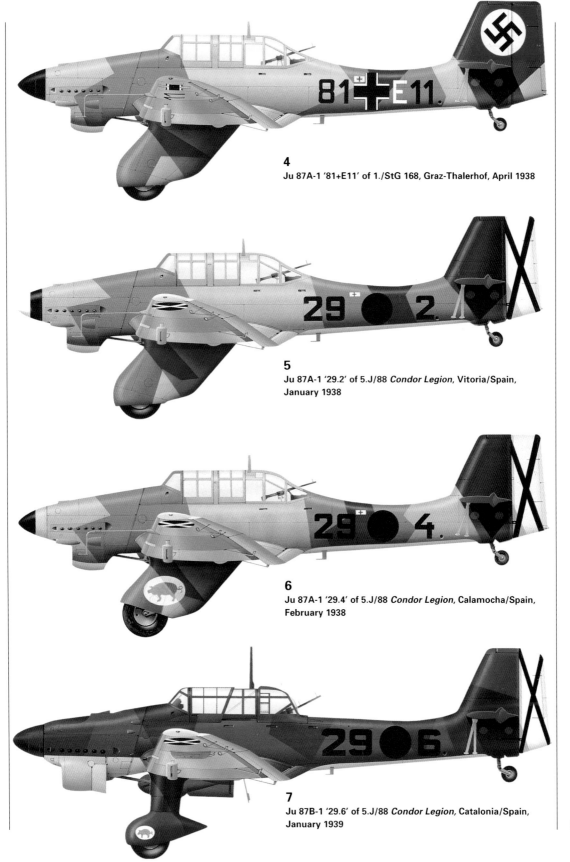

4
Ju 87A-1 '81+E11' of 1./StG 168, Graz-Thalerhof, April 1938

5
Ju 87A-1 '29.2' of 5.J/88 *Condor Legion*, Vitoria/Spain,
January 1938

6
Ju 87A-1 '29.4' of 5.J/88 *Condor Legion*, Calamocha/Spain,
February 1938

7
Ju 87B-1 '29.6' of 5.J/88 *Condor Legion*, Catalonia/Spain,
January 1939

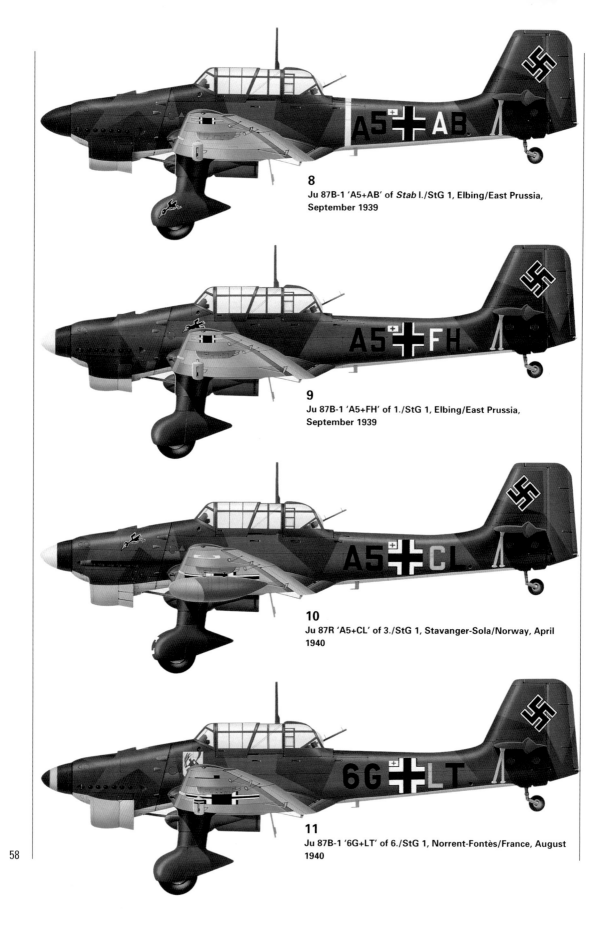

8
Ju 87B-1 'A5+AB' of *Stab* I./StG 1, Elbing/East Prussia,
September 1939

9
Ju 87B-1 'A5+FH' of 1./StG 1, Elbing/East Prussia,
September 1939

10
Ju 87R 'A5+CL' of 3./StG 1, Stavanger-Sola/Norway, April
1940

11
Ju 87B-1 '6G+LT' of 6./StG 1, Norrent-Fontès/France, August
1940

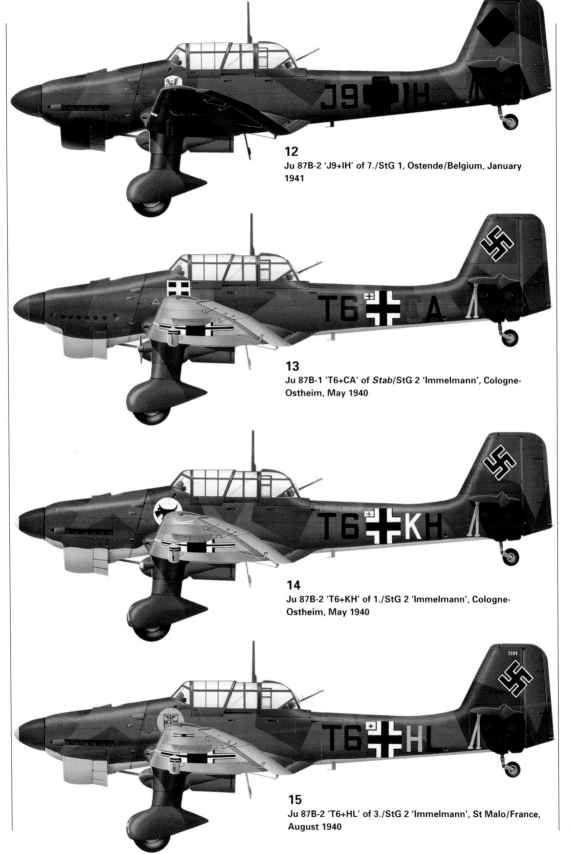

12
Ju 87B-2 'J9+IH' of 7./StG 1, Ostende/Belgium, January 1941

13
Ju 87B-1 'T6+CA' of *Stab*/StG 2 'Immelmann', Cologne-Ostheim, May 1940

14
Ju 87B-2 'T6+KH' of 1./StG 2 'Immelmann', Cologne-Ostheim, May 1940

15
Ju 87B-2 'T6+HL' of 3./StG 2 'Immelmann', St Malo/France, August 1940

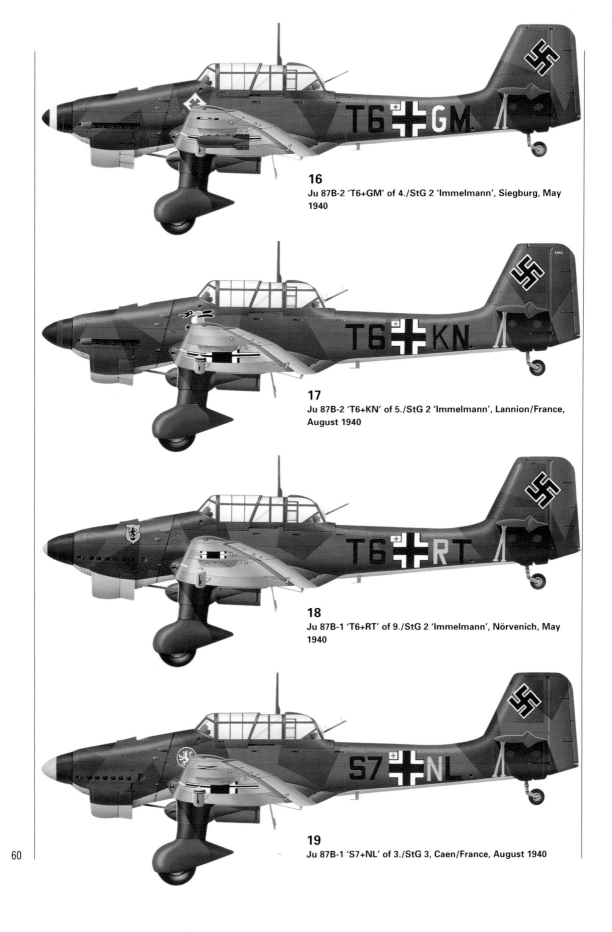

16
Ju 87B-2 'T6+GM' of 4./StG 2 'Immelmann', Siegburg, May
1940

17
Ju 87B-2 'T6+KN' of 5./StG 2 'Immelmann', Lannion/France,
August 1940

18
Ju 87B-1 'T6+RT' of 9./StG 2 'Immelmann', Nörvenich, May
1940

19
Ju 87B-1 'S7+NL' of 3./StG 3, Caen/France, August 1940

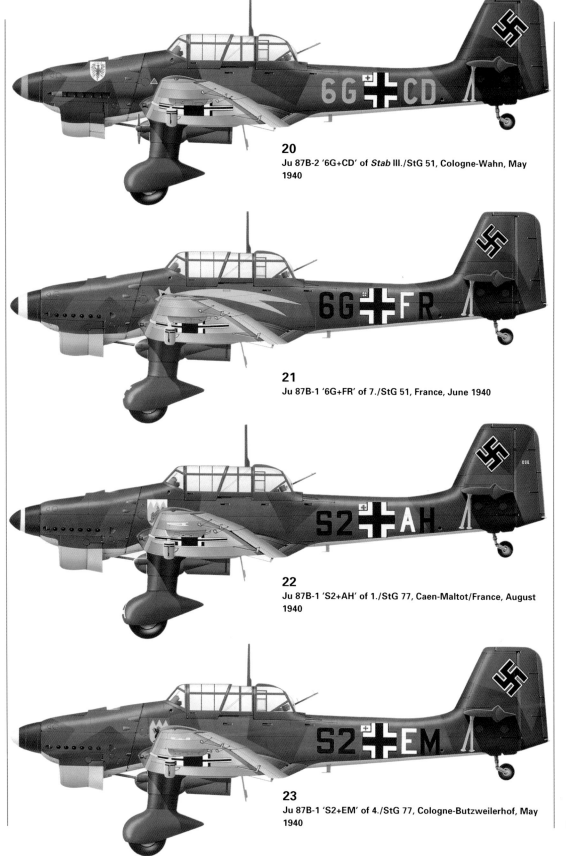

20
Ju 87B-2 '6G+CD' of *Stab* III./StG 51, Cologne-Wahn, May
1940

21
Ju 87B-1 '6G+FR' of 7./StG 51, France, June 1940

22
Ju 87B-1 'S2+AH' of 1./StG 77, Caen-Maltot/France, August
1940

23
Ju 87B-1 'S2+EM' of 4./StG 77, Cologne-Butzweilerhof, May
1940

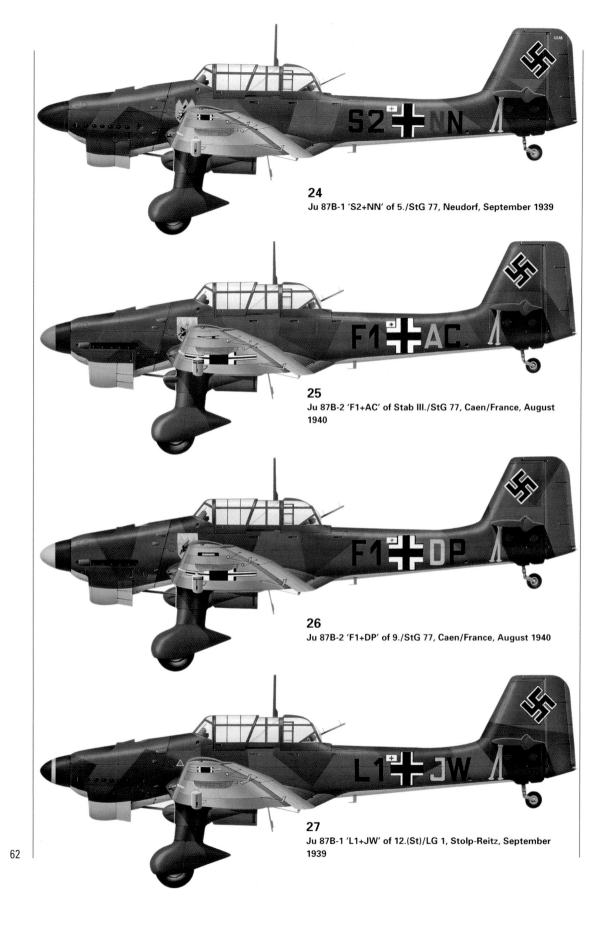

24
Ju 87B-1 'S2+NN' of 5./StG 77, Neudorf, September 1939

25
Ju 87B-2 'F1+AC' of Stab III./StG 77, Caen/France, August 1940

26
Ju 87B-2 'F1+DP' of 9./StG 77, Caen/France, August 1940

27
Ju 87B-1 'L1+JW' of 12.(St)/LG 1, Stolp-Reitz, September 1939

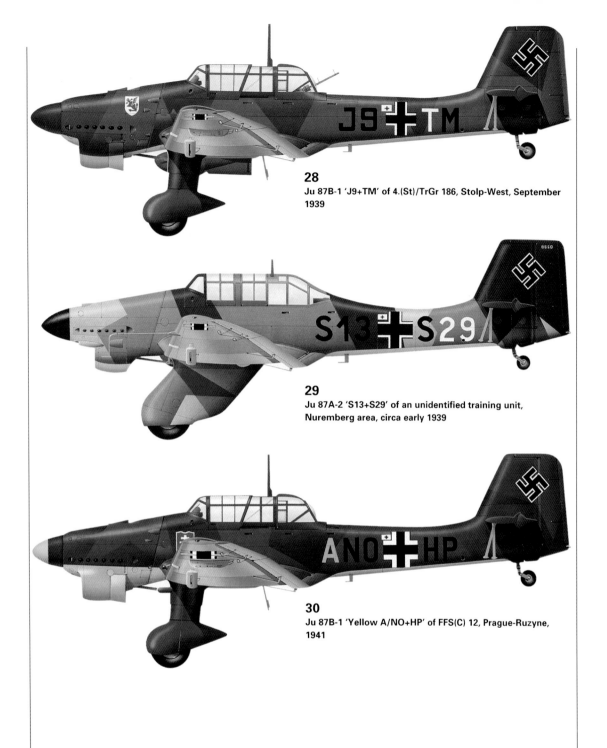

28
Ju 87B-1 'J9+TM' of 4.(St)/TrGr 186, Stolp-West, September 1939

29
Ju 87A-2 'S13+S29' of an unidentified training unit, Nuremberg area, circa early 1939

30
Ju 87B-1 'Yellow A/NO+HP' of FFS(C) 12, Prague-Ruzyne, 1941

1
Ju 87B-1 Oberleutnant Bruno Dilley,
Staffelkapitän of 3./StG 1 in
September 1939

2
Leutnant Hermann Haas was
Kettenführer of 5.J/88 in Spain in
January 1938

3
Major Oskar Dinort was *Geschwaderkommodore* of StG 2 between 1939
and 1941

4
Unteroffizier Gerhard Grenzel of
I./StG 1 is seen in Norway after win-
ning his Knight's Cross in May 1940

5
Oberst Günther Schwartzkopff was
Geschwaderkommodore of StG 77 in
France until his death on 15 May 1940

6
Major Clemens Graf von Schönborn-
Wiesentheid replaced Schwartzkopff,
and is seen here in late July 1940

THE MYTH IS EXPLODED

Having helped subjugate France in just six short weeks, the *Stuka-gruppen* were allowed precious little time to rest on their laurels. By the beginning of July von Richthofen had already established VIII. *Fliegerkorps* HQ at Deauville. The *Korps'* component *Gruppen* were deployed along the coastal areas of Normandy and Brittany to the west, and although a fortunate few were granted local leave to sample the delights of nearby French Channel resorts, home leave among the war weary aircrew was the exception rather than the rule.

One of the first reported encounters between Ju 87s and British shipping in this latest phase of the Stuka's operational career had been an ineffectual dive-bombing attack (believed to have been mounted by III./StG 51) on deep-sea convoy 'Jumbo', which was attacked whilst approaching Plymouth early on the afternoon of 1 July. Three Hurricane Is of No 213 Sqn were scrambled from Exeter to engage the Stukas, but by the time they had arrived over the convoy the raiders had long since departed.

Three days later III./StG 51 staged a maximum-effort raid on Portland harbour that resulted in probably the highest military loss of life ever inflicted by a single air attack on the British Isles. Led by their new *Kommandeur*, Hauptmann Anton Keil, some 33 Stukas dived out of the morning mist, which hung over the naval base, totally unannounced.

As a *Kette* lifts off in the background, 'Anton-Theodor' (aka 'G6+AT' of 9./StG 51) sits at dispersal fully bombed-up and awaiting its crew. The *Staffel* badge – a bomb-riding devil carrying a flaming torch – survived the unit's redesignation as 6./StG 1 early in July 1940, as too – for a while – did the original unit codes

They concentrated their attacks on the largest vessel in the harbour, the 5582-ton auxiliary anti-aircraft ship HMS *Foylebank*, and within eight minutes 22 bombs had struck the ship, killing 176 of her crew. Among them was Leading Seaman Jack Mantle who, despite being mortally wounded, continued to fire his two-pounder 'pom-pom' gun as the ship settled beneath him – an action which was recognised by the award of a posthumous VC on 3 September 1940.

With no RAF fighters in the vicinity, the *Gruppe* escaped back to Cherbourg all but unscathed, having also set fire to an oil tanker moored in Weymouth Bay with a direct hit from a 500-kg bomb prior to making good their escape – the vessel burned for 24 hours before the flames could be brought under control. The only loss inflicted upon the Ju 87s was one machine brought down over the target area, its wing blown off by a direct hit from one of the *Foylebank*'s 4-in anti-aircraft guns – both Leutnant Schwarz and his gunner were killed in the subsequent crash. A second Stuka landed back at Cherbourg having suffered minor flak damage.

The *Foylebank* episode was to be III./StG 51's swan-song, for five days later both Keil's *Gruppe* and I.(St)/TrGr 186 were redesignated to bring StG 1 up to full *Geschwader* establishment – the two *Gruppen* became II. and III./StG 1 respectively. Hauptmann Sigel's I./StG 76 also underwent a change of identity on this date. It now became I./StG 3, the first - and for the next 18 months only – *Gruppe* of the newly-planned *Stukageschwader* 3. This effectively left IV.(St)/LG 1 as the only semi-autonomous *Gruppe* operating the Ju 87, a status this unit would enjoy until its eventual redesignation as I./StG 5 early in 1942.

Whereas the above redesignations were little more than cosmetic (simply 'tidying up' the organisational framework without adding to its numbers), a completely new *Stukagruppe* had been activated on that same 9 July day. This was I./KG 76, a hitherto Do 17-equipped *Kampfgruppe* which, after conversion on to the Ju 87B, joined the ranks of the *Stukawaffe* as III./StG 77. The Luftwaffe thus entered upon the Battle of Britain which, from the Allied viewpoint, is deemed to have opened exactly 24 hours later on 10 July, with its Ju 87 strength increased to 11 *Gruppen* (although the poor serviceability returns of some units following the depredations of the recent weeks' fighting meant that the number of machines available was still roughly on a par with the campaigns in Poland and France – around the 300 mark).

StG 77 flew its first mission of the campaign on the eve of the 'official' battle when 27 aircraft of I. *Gruppe* took off from Théville late in the afternoon of 9 July to attack a convoy off Portland. They succeeded in damaging a small Ministry of Shipping vessel, but this time the Ju 87s were intercepted by three fighters – Spitfire Is of No 609 Sqn's Green Section, up from their nearby satellite airfield at Warmwell, the bulk of the unit being situated back at Middle Wallop. Engaged by the Stukas' escort of Bf 110Cs, the Spitfires claimed a solitary dive-bomber shot down.

The single kill fell to future ace Flg Off David M Crook (see Osprey volume *Aircraft of the Aces 12 Spitfire Mk I/II Aces 1939-41* for more details), who described the engagement in his autobiography *Spitfire Pilot*, published in June 1942;

'At about 6.30 pm we were ordered to patrol Weymouth, and so Peter (Flg Off Peter Drummond-Hay, who was killed in this action when over-

Hauptmann Anton Keil, *Gruppenkommandeur* of II./StG 1 (the ex-III./StG 51), is seen here wearing the Knight's Cross which was awarded to him on 19 August 1940. Keil remained at the head of II./StG 1 until he was killed on the Eastern Front a year later when his aircraft overturned during an emergency landing on swampy ground

Unlike Keil, Helmut Mahlke, who commanded III./StG 1 throughout the Battle of Britain and beyond, survived two crash landings in Russia. He is pictured here later in the war as an Oberstleutnant on the staff of *Luftflotte* 6

A Ju 87B-1 of StG 77 returns from a sortie with its underwing bomb-racks empty and the bomb cradle fork swinging freely in the slipstream. Note that this aircraft also appears to have a name written ahead of the *Staffel* badge – a not uncommon practice among Stuka units

whelmed by Bf 110 escorts), Michael (Plt Off Michael Appleby) and I took off, Peter leading. We circled round for about three-quarters of an hour, and saw nothing at all. Peter was getting very fed up with this apparently unnecessary flying, and we circled round the aerodrome and asked permission to land. We were told, however, to continue our patrol and turned out again over Weymouth at about 7000 ft. A moment later, looking out towards the left, I saw an aircraft dive into a layer of cloud about two miles away and then reappear. I immediately called up Peter on the RT, and he swung us into line astern, and turned left towards the enemy.

'A moment later I saw one or two more Huns appear, and recognised them as Junkers 87 dive-bombers. I immediately turned on my reflector sights, put my gun button on to "fire" and settled down to enjoy a little slaughter of a few Ju 87s, as they are rather helpless machines.'

Before Crook could indeed indulge in this, his first aerial combat, his section was bounced from above by the Bf 110 escorts. With cannon and tracer rounds visibly whizzing by overhead, Crook somehow managed to evade his attackers by breaking violently to port and then diving headlong into a bank of cloud below him, emerging on the other side with his Spitfire showing an indicated airspeed of over 400 mph.

As Crook broke into clear sky he spotted a Ju 87 immediately in front of him and fired a burst in its direction ('my first real shots of the war'), but the Stuka seemed to fly on oblivious to the Spitfire pilot's tracer rounds – although he was later credited with having damaged this Stuka, not a single Ju 87 returned to base with as much as a scratch. In the time it took Crook to turn around and commence a second attack, the dive-bomber had disappeared back into cloud.

After climbing back up to height and firing at a Bf 110, again with little effect, Crook spotted a second aircraft in cloud just nearby;

'At that moment I saw dimly a machine moving in the cloud on my left and flying parallel to me. I stalked him through the cloud, and when he emerged into a patch of clear sky I saw that it was Ju 87.

'I was in an ideal position to attack and opened fire and put the remainder of my ammunition – about 2000 rounds – into him at very close range. Even in the heat of the moment I well remember my amazement at the shattering effect of my fire. Pieces flew off his fuselage and cockpit covering, a stream of smoke appeared from the engine, and a moment later a great sheet of flame licked down out from the

With the pilot already aboard, groundcrew wait to start up the engine of this III./StG 2 'Immelmann' machine as the wireless-operator (left) apparently dashes back to the ops building for some forgotten item . . .

... all is well and the bomb-laden aircraft commence their widely spaced take-off runs. Many *Stukagruppen* paraded the unit standard and provided a ceremonial honour-guard such as seen here at the beginning of each operational mission

engine cowling and he dived down vertically. The flames enveloped the whole machine and he went straight down, apparently quite slowly, for about 5000 ft, till he was just a shapeless burning mass of wreckage.

'Absolutely fascinated by the sight, I followed him down, and saw him hit the sea with a great burst of white foam. He disappeared immediately, and apart from a green patch in the water there was no sign that anything had happened. The crew made no attempt to get out, and they were obviously killed in my first burst of fire.'

David Crook's premier combat victory had inflicted a grievous blow to I./StG 77, for the aircraft shot down into the Channel some 20 kilometres south-southwest of Portland was being piloted by their *Kommandeur*, Hauptmann Friedrich-Karl *Freiherr* von Dalwigk zu Lichtenfels. Another of the Stuka arm's 'Old Guard', he had joined the then StG 162 'Immelmann' back in 1936. Assuming command of I./StG 77 shortly before the outbreak of war, he had personally flown at the head of the *Gruppe* on almost every one of its missions since. His 'leadership by example' throughout the Polish and French campaigns was to result in the posthumous award of the Knight's Cross and his promotion to Major.

Forty-eight hours later the Stukas were back over Portland. A ten-aircraft strong sortie despatched from the Cherbourg peninsula early on the morning of 11 July had attacked a convoy in Lyme Bay, sunk one of the escort (HMS Warrior II, a 36-year-old armed yacht) and returned without loss thanks to the efforts of their Bf 109E escorts, who downed two Spitfire Is (of No 609 Sqn again) and a solitary Hurricane I (of No 501 Sqn) during the course of the mission. No doubt encouraged by this, the *Gruppe* staged a second mission a few hours later, which comprised a mixed formation of some 20 'Bertas' and 'Richards' of III./StG 2, escorted by twice that number of Bf 110Cs from III./ZG 76. The Stukas had just completed their dives against a convoy off Portland, and were at their most vulnerable, when they were intercepted at low-level by six Hurricane Is of No 601 Sqn, which had been scrambled from Tangmere, some 50 miles further east.

Again, the RAF fighters arrived too late to stop the Stukas from completing their attack, and just one machine would fail to return, having been sent crashing into the water alongside Portland mole after being attacked by Flg Off G N S Cleaver, who also claimed a He 111 near Portsmouth on this date – a pre-war member of the British Olympic Skiing team, as well as a keen Auxiliary pilot with No 601 'County of London' Sqn, 'Mouse' Cleaver was awarded a DFC in September 1940, having destroyed seven aircraft, plus claimed a further two as probables. No less than four of the Bf 110 escorts were lost as they fought a bitter rearguard action in the Stukas' wake against a number of Hurricanes sent to reinforce No 601 Sqn.

While VIII.*Fliegerkorps* was thus directing its attention against the

As the port wingman closes up on his leader, the badge of III.*Gruppe* (the Hlinka Cros of Slovakia, bestowed by the local population during the unit's brief sojourn at Vienne the previous autumn) is clearly apparent

III./StG 2 'Immelmann' was heavily involved in the western Channel convoy actions of mid-July. This small coaster has had a lucky escape, as witness the rings in the water marking a succession of near misses

Dorset coast and the western end of the Channel, the two *Stukagruppen* now subordinated to *Luftflotte* 2 and based to the east in the Pas de Calais were awaiting the opportunity to attack across the Channel's narrowest point – the Straits of Dover.

Their chance came on 13 July when reports were received of a convoy attempting to run the gauntlet of the Straits. In contrast to von Richthofen's Normandy-based *Gruppen*, whose cross-Channel sorties could last over an hour, and invariably involved a round-trip of some 275 kilometres or more, the single *Staffel* of II./StG 1 despatched that day had but a quarter of that distance to cover. Such short-range missions had one other great advantage – they could be provided with an escort of single-engined Bf 109s. The benefit of such cover was amply demonstrated during the first foray against the Dover convoy. While a bitter dogfight raged between the three *Staffeln* of Bf 109Es from JG 51 and 11 Hurricane Is of No 56 Sqn, the Stukas managed to deliver their ordnance and then escape without loss, although two machines received slight damage – in an early example of the overclaiming that was to plague Fighter Command during the Battle of Britain, the Hurricane squadron (who lost two pilots to the Bf 109 escort) claimed to have shot down seven Ju 87s during the course of this sortie.

Twenty-four hours later an attack on a convoy off Eastbourne by all three *Staffeln* of IV.(St)/LG 1 fared less well, with one Stuka (flown by Oberleutnant Sonnberg) and one of the escorting Bf 109s being lost to RAF fighters – the Ju 87 was claimed by three No 615 Sqn pilots, two of whom, Flg Offs P Collard and P Hugo, would go on to become aces.

Nearly a week was to pass before II./StG 1 reappeared off the Kent coast. In the early evening of 20 July they attacked an eastbound convoy, code-named 'Bosom', as it approached the Straits of Dover. Once again a strong fighter escort (over 50 Bf 109s and Bf 110s) proved its worth, for despite being bounced out of the sun by Hurricane Is of Nos 32 and 615 Sqns, plus Spitfire Is of Nos 65 and 610 Sqn, all Hauptmann Keil's pilots again made it safely back to France (albeit this time with four aircraft damaged and one gunner wounded – the Hurricane pilots claimed to have downed two Stukas), having sunk the coaster *Pulborough* and left the destroyer HMS *Brazen* with her back broken. The fighter escorts

faired less well, however, losing five Bf 109Es in a swirling dogfight that lasted over 30 minutes.

Five days later the Stukas suffered their first multiple losses of the Battle when missions were flown over both ends of the Channel. Between Dover and Folkestone a series of heavy attacks on a westbound convoy by units of *Luftflotte* 2, including II./StG 1 and IV.(St)/LG 1, sank five ships and damaged four others, including the destroyers *Boreas* and *Brilliant*. A pilot of II./StG 1 described the scene;

'The French coast slips away behind us. While our fighter escort banks and turns all around us we keep in tight formation, heading out over the gently rolling sea towards our target. The first faint outline of England is already visible when we locate the remains of the convoy. A few scattered ships are trying to reach the safety of that far shore. Our comrades who were here before us have done their job well. Only eight ships are still above water.

'The *Kommandeur* gives the pre-arranged signal to attack. Ahead of me one machine after the other wings over and disappears into its vertical dive. I am just about to follow suit when an English fighter closes in on me. I quickly stand my crate on its head and succeed in shaking him off. While my wireless-operator watches him and keeps up a running commentary on his movements, I concentrate on the ship I have selected as my target. It looms larger in my sights by the second. A slight pressure on the release button – a jolt – and my bomb is on its way.

'Looking back, I see it explode alongside the ship's hull. But the aircraft behind me scores a direct hit. There is no time to bask in our success – despite the best efforts of our fighter escort, enemy fighters have broken through and are trying to pick us off one by one. Diving out of the sun's glare they have caught a

Above left
This IV.(St)/LG 1 B-1 has a small individual aircraft letter ('F' or 'P'?) repeated on both wheelspats

Above
IV.(St)/LG 1's badge – although the bomb appears to have been stencilled on to the pale blue shield, the red devil itself and the elaborate white 'L' (for *Lehrgeschwader*) are amateurish in the extreme

At the other end of the Channel the aircraft of 5./StG 2 'Immelmann' were identified by this rather aggressive penguin. The reason the *Staffel* opted for a flightless bird as its emblem is not clear. No mystery about the triangle at the lower right though. It indicates the type of fuel to be used – E87 = *Einheitsstreibstoff 87 Oktan* (Standard 87 Octane Fuel)

comrade ahead of me broadside on. Although his machine is already in flames he climbs briefly to give himself and his operator a chance to bale out. Seconds later his aircraft disappears in a column of spray.

'My own operator reports two fighters approaching. One sits on my tail while the other remains off high to one side. With one wingtip almost touching the water I bank to evade the fire from the first while my observer looses off at the second. They break away for another pass, but in the meantime I quickly tuck myself in behind a gaggle of comrades ahead of me as we head for home at full throttle.'

Two II./StG 1 machines were lost in this action and a third – of IV.(St)/LG 1 – was damaged. Meanwhile, elements of VIII. *Fliegerkorps* to the west had returned yet again to Portland. After the raid III./StG 1 was chased back across the Channel by RAF fighters. They suffered two aircraft damaged and one lost, the latter shot into the sea by two No 152 Sqn Spitfire Is just before reaching the safety of Cherbourg.

Forty-eight hours later a machine of I./StG 77 failed to return from a 30 Stuka-strong attack on convoy 'Bacon' steaming east off Portland – it was shot down into Weymouth Bay by future Hurricane ace Plt Off C T Davis of No 238 Sqn. On this same day the Royal Navy lost two more destroyers to air attack (HMSs *Codrington* and *Wren*), forcing it to withdraw its Dover flotilla to safer waters.

On 29 July the two *Stukagruppen* of *Luftflotte* 2 (48 Ju 87s in all, escorted by some eighty Bf 109s) launched a heavy early-morning raid on shipping in Dover harbour. For one young wireless-operator it was quite an introduction to operational flying;

'A thick morning mist separates the sleeping earth 5000 metres below from our machines as we head for the Channel in *Staffel* formation. All that is visible is the occasional glimmer from a stream or pond catching and reflecting the first rays of the rising sun. We fly a wide loop out over the French coast as our fighter escort climbs up out of the mist to join us.

'The pilot's voice is steady and reassuring to a tyro like myself: "Off to the left in front of us the Channel, in the distance the English coast". Now it's directly under our wings, the shimmering blue-violet surface of the

Also active over the western Channel, two B-2s of StG 77 return to Normandy after yet another mission off the Dorset coast

Channel, lightly ruffled by the morning breeze. But this is no time to be admiring the beauties of nature.

'"*Achtung!* Prepare to dive." says the calm voice in the headphones. "Ready!" I reply. I grip the butt of my machine-gun with both hands and brace my feet against the cabin floor supports. A quick glance to check the seat straps, parachute harness and the position of the emergency lever in the roof which has to be pulled to release the canopy. And now "*Hals und Beinbruch*" – we're going into the dive!

'I am pressed down in my seat by a tremendous weight . . . for several seconds a dark red veil comes down in front of my eyes, but then the pilot starts to pull out. The most dangerous moment of the entire mission.

'Our machine presents the whole length of its vulnerable belly to the English flak gunners, who are shooting at us with weapons of every calibre. The shells burst all around us leaving little clouds of black cotton wool hanging in the sky.

'Above the chalk cliffs German and English fighters are embroiled in a wild dogfight. Off to the right over open water a machine plunges down almost vertically. Just as it seems about to smash itself into pieces it levels out only a few metres above the "drink", turns steeply and heads straight for our Stuka. The rounded wings of the aircraft betray its nationality: "English fighter behind us to port", I scream at the pilot. "What?" – I must have yelled too loudly. I repeat my warning in a quieter voice. The pilot yanks our machine over onto its side. With one movement I release the safety on my machine gun and let fly, but the Spitfire has left his attack too late. As we near the protection of the German coastal batteries he breaks off and heads back towards Dover.

'All aircraft of our *Staffel* return safely from their morning visit to England. Teddy, our *Staffel* mascot, greets each of us by barking excitedly as we climb wearily out of our machines.'

But three Stukas did not make it back, having fallen victim to Spitfire Is of No 41 Sqn and Hurricane Is of No 501 Sqn, whilst another Ju 87 was written off in a crash-landing back in France. That same day HM destroyer *Delight* was sent to the bottom off Portland.

The weather deteriorated as July drew to a close, but the *Stukagruppen* had already performed to perfection the initial task required of them in the run-up to the planned invasion of England. By 'plugging' the Channel at either end, and neutralising the Royal Navy's south coast destroyer flotillas (which had lost a dozen vessels since mid-May, plus many others withdrawn from the area for essential repairs), they had secured the cross-Channel sealanes for the invasion fleet, which was even now being assembled in northern European ports.

Next would come stages two and three of their part in the conquest of Great Britain. In August – repeating the tactics of Poland and France – they would take out RAF Fighter Command's forward airfields in a series of precision attacks in preparation for the landings. And in September, once the German army was safely ashore, they would resume their classic role of 'flying artillery' as the ground-troops pushed northwards into the heart of England. The relative ease with which they had accomplished phase one (at a cost of only some dozen aircraft lost or written off) had given no indication of the storm that was about to break over them.

On 8 August, however, the last major convoy action of the Battle afforded a grim foretaste of things to come. Convoy CW 9 (code-named 'Peewit'), comprising 20 merchantmen and nine naval escorts, had sailed from the Medway the previous evening, but before dawn three of its number had already been sunk by E-boats in the Straits of Dover – its progress having been tracked by the recently-installed *Freya* radar site situated on the Calais coast. As it ploughed westwards along the Channel, it was subjected to two Stuka attacks.

The first, by elements of StG 1, was intercepted and broken up by six squadrons of RAF fighters, who claimed two Ju 87s destroyed and two damaged – all these claims (plus three against Bf 109Es) were submitted by No 145 Sqn, who in turn had lost two Hurricane Is to the Stukas' escort, provided on this occasion by I./JG 27. By early afternoon 'Peewit' was off the Isle of Wight, where it was attacked by some 60 Stukas of I. and III./StG 2, backed up by I./StG 3. Despite the intervention of more fighters (18 Hurricane Is from Nos 145, 238 and 257 Sqns, plus Spitfire Is in strength from No 609 Sqn), this time the Stukas got through to the ships and sunk four and damaged seven, but lost a trio of aircraft (all from I./StG 3), with a further four suffering varying degrees of damage – two of the Ju 87s again fell to No 145 Sqn, whilst the third was claimed by No 609 Sqn. One Bf 110C of V./LG 1 and three Bf 109Es of III./JG 27 had also been lost, but they had exacted a heavy toll on the attacking Hurricane units, No 257 Sqn losing three pilots killed and No 238 Sqn two.

Flying with No 609 Sqn on this occasion was Flg Off D M Crook, who succinctly described the weather conditions on the day of this engagement in the following extract from his autobiography;

'On 8th August, soon after dawn, we were ordered to patrol a convoy off the Needles. It was a very clear day with a brilliant sun – just the sort of day that the Germans love, because they come out at a very big height and dive down to attack out of the sun. By doing this cleverly, they used to render themselves almost invisible until the attack was delivered. We hated these clear days and always prayed for high cloud to cover the sun.'

As the scattered survivors of the convoy regrouped south of the Isle of Wight and made course for Weymouth Bay, von Richthofen despatched yet a third wave of his Stukas to finish them off. This time it was the turn of the Caen-based StG 77;

'The *Staffelkapitäne* were ordered to report to the *Kommandeur*. A quarter of an hour later the hooter begins to sound: the signal for the start of an operational mission. The chief briefly explains the situation. "Enemy convoy south-east of the Isle of Wight. Full *Geschwader* attack. *Staffeln* and *Ketten* to seek their own targets of opportunity – take-off at 16.30 hours."

'We quickly plot our course. There are no points of orientation over open water and so we'll have to fly strictly according to the compass. Everybody gets ready. The most important item of clothing is the life-jacket. Shortly before 16.00 hours the whole *Geschwader* is assembled and ready for take-off. Our *Stabskette* is to lead. A brief hand signal and, like a flock of birds, one *Staffel* after the other, one *Gruppe* after the other, we take to the air. We circle, get into formation, and head for the Channel.

'Within a few minutes we reach the cost. Ahead of us, as far as the eye can see, stretches the Channel – once the busiest shipping lane in the world, today the largest ships' graveyard.

'Water - nothing but water below us . . . until there! Cautiously, you could say almost shyly, a light strip emerges from the green-blue waters. Scarcely visible at first. The south coast of England. A few hundred metres above us are several *Staffeln* of our escort – fighters (Bf 109Es of II. and III./JG 27) and *Zerstörer* (V./LG 1). And ahead, off to the right and at an altitude of some 3000 to 4000 metres, the first dogfights are already beginning to develop. It is hard to tell friend from foe. All we can make out are small silver specks tumbling about the sky. Time to be especially alert. The enemy coastline draws ever nearer, down below to our left the Isle of Wight. And then – 10 or 12 ships. They have spotted us and are starting to zig-zag. We turn to approach from the east. Suddenly a voice over the W/T: "Aircraft Four emergency landing". An Unteroffizier of 4.*Staffel* is going down – hope he makes it safely (probably Unteroffizier Pittroff, who force-landed at St Lawrence on the Isle of Wight, having been attacked by No 145 Sqn ace, Plt Off Peter Parrott – Pittroff was made a PoW, but his wireless operator, Unteroffizier Schubert, was killed in the initial attack – Ed).

'"*Puma 1* to all *Pumas*. Attack!" We are right over the convoy – it seems to be all small ships. The *Ketten* separate and each selects a target which has not yet been hit. Our leading *Kette* starts its dive close inshore. But what's this? Four aircraft? I can't believe my eyes – the third *Kette*, attacking off to my left, the same picture. At that moment I hear over the headphones: "*Puma. Achtung!* Enemy fighters from above – diving with us!"

'But during the dive our machines are also banking to keep the targets in their sights. The *Engländer* can hardly get a shot in and – because of their greater speed – have to pull out earlier, leaving us to concentrate on our aiming. I lead my *Kette* down on the southernmost ship, having first checked with my wireless-operator that there is nothing on our tail; "All clear, Herr Oberleutnant". We don't use our dive-brakes. In this sort of situation – the most important thing is to get back into formation

'Like a flock of huge birds' – a *Staffel* lifts off virtually as one to carry the fight to England's shores

quickly. My bomb lands close alongside the ship, the *Kettenhund's* on the left is a near miss too. But the third member of our trio is bang on target; a hit amidships. After a few seconds flames erupt from the vessel, followed by huge clouds of smoke. We leave her dead in the water, listing badly.

'Now they're onto us, the *Engländer*. Spitfires, Hurricanes. From a distance it's hard to distinguish them from our own Me's. A fierce dogfight rages over the Isle of Wight. Some 60 aircraft of all types, German and English, in a life or death struggle. Several of the *Engländer* make for the mainland trailing smoke. To my right a 109 goes down into the sea; the pilot manages to bail out just in time. An unidentified machine circles above us totally enveloped in flames. It explodes and falls from the sky in tiny fragments – the only recognisable pieces are the wings.

'The *Engländer* keep at us. We reform and head southwards. We weave and turn constantly to escape the enemy's eight machine-guns. Our wireless-operators fire like men possessed. Again and again the British attack us from astern. Several times I hear the sound of bullets striking my machine. But the engine is not hit, it continues to run quietly and evenly. The closer we get to mid-Channel the fewer *Engländer* still attacking us. The *Staffeln* have gradually regained formation. The 4.*Staffel* is off to our left. One of their machines is trailing smoke. Its pilot radios: "Aircraft damaged - ditching". At that moment a Spitfire approaches it head-on, fires, scores a number of hits, and the Stuka crashes into the sea. A brief wall of spray, and then the waters of the Channel close over the spot. He's done for. Nothing we can do to help here.

'Half an hour later the Normandy coast comes into view. We all breathe a sigh of relief. My two *Kettenhunde* close up on me, waving and smiling. Our *Staffel* appears to be all present and correct as we land back at base. We have indeed all returned safely, although some aircraft have as many as 40 bullet holes in them. After an hour the chief returns, looking very serious. "The *Kommandeur* is missing. Hauptmann Schmack and Unteroffizier Pittroff too". We can't believe it. Nobody saw the *Kommandeur* crash. He was still with the *Stabskette* after the attack. After that, no-one knows anything.'

In fact, Hauptmann Waldemar Plewig's aircraft was shot into the sea by Hurricane Is of No 145 Sqn, one of three Ju 87s credited to the unit in this, its third and final battle with the Stukas over 'Peewit' on 8 August – the squadron also claimed a Bf 109E-4 of 5./JG 27, but had lost three

A *'Berta'* of 7./StG 77, its bomb racks empty, reaches the safety of the Normandy coast. Note the two machines, just visible background left, peeling off to land

pilots killed by the Messerschmitt escorts. No 145 Sqn had lost five pilots during its day-long battle with the *Stukageschwader*, and their escorts, over the convoy, but had claimed 21 enemy aircraft destroyed – their actual score was more likely to have been 11 destroyed and seven damaged. In recognition of their efforts, messages of congratulation flooded into their Westhampnett base from the Chief of Air Staff, AOC No 11 Group and the Secretary of State for Air, plus the remnants of the unit were visited later that very day in the field by HRH The Duke of Gloucester.

As No 145 Sqn's most distinguished victim on 8 August, Hauptmann Plewig had actually managed to escape his stricken Ju 87 before it crashed into the sea (his wireless operator was not so fortunate) and was rescued by one of the convoy's escort vessels. Made a prisoner-of-war when he was put ashore, Plewig was awarded the Knight's Cross some four months later. The medal was forwarded to him in captivity, and formal presentation was made by the CO of Shap Wells PoW camp in January 1941!

Of the 20 ships which had sailed from the Medway the previous night, only four arrived in Swanage virtually unscathed. The day's action had cost the four participating *Stukageschwader* nine aircraft lost or written off, plus a further ten damaged. By contrast, an attack by *Luftflotte 2*'s two *Stukagruppen* on vessels within convoy 'Booty' off Clacton some 72 hours later resulted in their losing just one machine apiece – kills split between Nos 74 (Spitfire I) and 151 (Hurricane I) Sqns.

This latter, relatively minor, skirmish of 11 August may not in itself have been very significant in the overall scheme of the Battle, but it was to mark the start of the last week of the Stuka's operational career – and reputation – as a potent force in the skies of north-west Europe.

13 August 1940 will forever be known as '*Adlertag*' ('Eagle Day') – the opening round of the Luftwaffe's main air assault on the British Isles. For the protagonists, their 'big day' did not get off to a good start for adverse weather conditions in the early morning led to last-minute postponement orders being transmitted. But not all units received them, and in the resulting confusion some bombers flew missions devoid of fighter cover, while other fighters dutifully flew to assigned target areas without the bombers they were meant to protect!

By the afternoon, however, the weather had improved sufficiently to allow the *Stukagruppen* to launch the second phase of their three-part role in the overall invasion plan – a series of pinpoint attacks intended to neutralise Fighter Command's forward fields. They struck along both flanks of the designated assault zone. In the east *Luftflotte* 2 despatched II./StG 1 against Rochester and IV.(St)/LG 1 against Detling. The former failed to locate their target, but Hauptmann von Brauchitsch's 40 Ju 87s caused severe damage at Detling, killing 67 (including the station commander Grp Capt Edward Davis), demolishing the hangars and totally destroying 22 aircraft. Retiring without loss, IV.(St)/LG 1 landed back at Tramecourt with justifiable feelings of a job well done. It was German intelligence which was at fault – Detling was not a Fighter Command airfield.

Indeed, the only aircraft permanently based there were Anson Is of No 500 'County of Kent' Sqn, which had been seconded to Coastal Command since early 1939. One of the unit's armourers provided this candid description of the oncoming raid as seen from his squadron dispersal;

'The B Flight night-duty groundcrew finished their evening meal and waited in and around the Dennis lorry which would take them to the Anson aircraft, parked in fields alongside the Yelsted road at the north-east corner of Detling aerodrome.

'Faintly, in the distance, Maidstone's air-raid shelter sirens were heard, and then the drone of aircraft. These aircraft could be seen approaching the airfield from about two miles away to the south-east at a height of

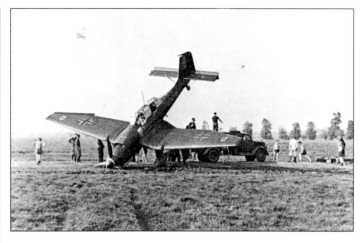

The spells of unseasonable August weather played havoc with many of the Luftwaffe's ill-prepared forward landing grounds. I./StG 77 at le Mesul-Angat, in Normandy, did not escape their share of trouble, 1.*Staffel*'s 'Dora-Heinrich' ending up on its nose after digging in a wheel upon its return from an attack on southern England. In Luftwaffe parlance, this somewhat undignified position was known as a '*Flieger-denkmal*' ('Airman's monument')

about 5000 ft. The formation was much larger than had been seen in the area before – so much so that it prompted one of the squadron armourers, Bill Yates, to announce that he "didn't know we had so many". This remark almost qualified for "Famous last words" as Yates clambered to the Dennis' canvas top and began a count of the aircraft. He had passed the 30 mark when the leading machine dipped its port wing in a diving turn, and became without any shadow of a doubt a Stuka.'

To the west units of VIII.*Fliegerkorps* suffered similar diversities of fortune. Elements of StG 77 searched in vain for Warmwell before dropping their bombs at random over the Dorset countryside and returning to their Caen airfields unmolested. Despite being bereft of fighter cover (their 30 Bf 109 escorts from II./JG 53 had been obliged to turn back through a shortage of fuel), Hauptmann Walter Enneccerus' 27 II./StG 2 Ju 87Rs crossed the coast near Lyme Regis en route for Middle Wallop but they never made it. Intercepted by 13 Spitfire Is of No 609 Sqn, they lost five of their number in a one-sided duel over the coast, and a sixth which crashed into the Channel during the return flight – the RAF claimed to have destroyed or damaged 14 Ju 87s and Bf 109s and suffered no losses.

This decimation of the Stukas had been witnessed from the Portland cliffs by Prime Minister Winston Churchill and a clutch of senior Army generals. One of the pilots to claim a Ju 87 destroyed, and a second dive-bomber damaged, was leading No 609 Sqn ace, Flg Off John Dundas;

'Thirteen Spitfires left Warmwell for a memorable Tea-time party over Lyme Bay, and an unlucky day for the species Ju 87, of which no less than 14 suffered destruction or damage in a record squadron "bag", which also included five of the escorting Me's. The formation, consisting of about 40 dive-bombers in four-vic formation, with about as many Me 110s and 109s stepped-up above them, was surprised by 609's down-sun attack.'

The four-minute massacre off the Dorset coast was widely reported in the contemporary press, with the following headline from the 14 August 1940 edition of *The Times* being typical of those which appeared in a number of national dailies on this date;

'All the nine Junkers were brought down . . . by a single Spitfire squadron, as well as four Me 109s. This same squadron had brought down seven enemy aircraft the previous day.'

On that same 14 August *Luftflotte* 2's two *Stukagruppen* (some 80 aircraft in all, escorted by all three *Gruppen* of JG 26) again approached the Kent coast. Four RAF fighter squadrons (Hurricane Is of Nos 32 and 615 Sqns and Spitfire Is of Nos 65 and 610 Sqns – a total of 42 aircraft), alerted by radar, were waiting for them. At such short range the Messerschmitt pilots of JG 26 were able to stay and mix it, resulting in a massive dogfight involving over 200 machines developing over the coast between Dover and Folkestone. Unable to penetrate inland, the Stukas had no option but to withdraw, escaping the melée with one aircraft shot down (a 10./LG 1 machine, destroyed by a No 615 Sqn Hurricane I) and another damaged. Two *Ketten* did, however, vent their frustration on their way back to Tramecourt by bombing and sinking the unarmed Goodwin lightship. Their Bf 109 escorts were credited with destroying four British fighters for the loss a single aircraft.

Twenty-four hours later the two *Gruppen* did get through to their assigned targets. Attacking

Just visible to left of centre, the white column of water at the foot of the cliffs reportedly indicates a near miss on a British cliff-top anti-aircraft emplacement. Despite some distinctive features, it has not yet been possible to identify the exact location

Hawkinge, IV.(St)/LG 1 lost two machines to the resident Hurricane Is of No 501 Sqn, 11 of which had been scrambled some 30 minutes earlier. Although this attack had been intercepted just as the Stukas were forming up into their pre-dive echelon, the 26 Ju 87s of II./StG 1 struck the forward field of Lympne totally unopposed. Both *Gruppen* had made extensive use of smaller 50-kg fragmentation bombs, which were obviously intended to destroy aircraft on the ground without rendering the fields themselves unserviceable for their own future use. This time faulty intelligence could not be blamed for the fact that there were no aircraft on the ground at either airfield at the time of the attacks.

Later that same afternoon VIII.*Fliegerkorps* returned to its old stamping grounds when some 40 Ju 87Rs of I./StG 1 and II./StG 2, with a heavy escort of 60 Bf 109Es from JGs 27 and 53 and 20 Bf 110Cs from V./LG 2, set out for Portland. Engaged by Hurricane Is from No 87 and 213 Sqns and Spitfire Is from No 234 Sqn, it was again II./StG 2 which bore the brunt of the losses, three of their aircraft failing to return against I./StG 1's single casualty – three of these kills were credited to No 87 Sqn and one to No 213.

So far in this, their final week of the Battle, the Stukas had failed in their objective of forcing the RAF's fighters to abandon their forward fields. But then neither had their own losses (with the exception of Hauptmann Enneccerus' unfortunate II./StG 2) been particularly heavy. The next 72 hours were to prove very different.

On 16 August it was I. and III./StG 2 which led a midday raid of over 100 aircraft (including Bf 109E escorts from II./JG 2) towards the eastern tip of the Isle of Wight. Approaching the Foreland, flares from the leading machine signalled the formation to split. While two *Ketten* of Ju 87s peeled away to port to attack the CH (Chain Home) radar station at Ventnor on the island itself (which had already been damaged by Ju 88s four days earlier), and I./StG 3 headed across Spithead towards the naval air station at Lee-on-Solent, the main body held course north-eastwards for the Fighter Command sector station at Tangmere.

Although most of the field's fighters had been scrambled, they were unable to prevent the two StG 2 *Gruppen* from carrying out a 'textbook attack'. Screaming down out of the sun high overhead, Stuka after Stuka planted its bombs with unerring accuracy. Every one of Tangmere's hangars was hit in succession, together with many of the station's other buildings and stores. A number of fighters under repair were also written off, and all eight aircraft of the nocturnal Fighter Interception Unit - seven radar-equipped Blenheims and the RAF's first Beaufighter night-fighter - were reportedly either destroyed or damaged. Twenty service and civilian personnel died amid the devastation.

The defending fighters (Hurricane Is from Nos 1, 43 and 601 Sqns and Spitfire Is of No 602 Sqn) may not have been able to forestall the onslaught, but they caught the Stukas at their most vulnerable – while recovering, attempting to regroup and trying to make good their escape. Three I. *Gruppe* Ju 87s were quickly downed by No 43 Sqn, whilst twice that number (mainly from III./StG 2) were destroyed over the Channel, the last just short of the Normandy coast. As many again, and more, were damaged, four returning to France with dead or wounded aircrew aboard (included amongst this number was a solitary I./StG 3 aircraft).

It had been a salutary lesson. The lack of a 'hostile airspace' in Spain, and the dearth of organised, and sustained, fighter opposition since, had ill-prepared the Stuka's supporters within the Luftwaffe High Command for the losses which their much-vaunted 'flying artillery' was now begin-ning to suffer in its new, longer-range, role. Even its staunchest advocates were having to concede that the Stuka was not operable as a strategic weapon if pitted against a determined defence – on the Tangmere raid, the Spitfire pilots of No 602 Sqn had kept the Bf 109 escorts fully occu-pied whilst the Hurricane units tackled the Ju 87s. It would take just one more reversal to write *finis* to its career in the west. And that reversal – even bloodier than the aftermath of Tangmere – was just 48 hours away.

After the heightened activity of the previous two days, 17 August pro-vided a welcome lull. By day, the Luftwaffe restricted itself to reconnais-sance flights, and the only combat loss was a night-intruder Ju 88 of 4./NJG 1, shot down off the Humber by a No 29 Sqn Blenheim during the early hours of the morning.

Tonneville/Cherbourg, 18 August 1940. Wireless-operator/gunner Unteroffizier Heinz Sellhorn of I./StG 77 uses an SC 250 bomb as a convenient seat to catch up on some reading as he awaits the order to board his aircraft for the ill-fated attack on Thorney Island

However, on Sunday, 18 August, the Luftwaffe was back with a vengeance in one final attempt to destroy Fighter Command. Once again the main objectives were air-fields, with a lesser effort being directed against the radar stations. And on this, the 'Hardest Day' of the entire Battle, none was hit harder than Major von Schönborn-Wiesentheid's *Stukageschwader 77*.

All three *Gruppen* were involved, I. and II./StG 77 (28 Stukas apiece) targeting the airfields at Thorney Island and Ford respectively, whilst III. *Gruppe* (31 aircraft) was assigned the Poling CH radar station. Rein-forcing them, I./StG 3 (22 Ju 87s) was to attack the airfield at Gosport. The four *Gruppen* assembled above Cherbourg at 13.45 and then set

Part of the *Gruppe* which led the disastrous 18 August raid. Both of the aircraft pictured here ('Julius' and 'Ludwig' respectively – see individual letters on the machines' wheelspats) belonged to 7./StG 77 assigned to attack Poling Chain Home radar station

course northwards to rendezvous with a strong escort of Bf 109E fighters (70 from JG 27 and 32 from JG 53). This was largest complement of Ju 87s (109 in total) yet seen over Britain. III./StG 77 led the way, at its head *Gruppenkommandeur* Hauptmann Helmut Bode who, having begun his flying career as a long-range maritime reconnaissance pilot, barely gave the 120-kilometre cross-Channel hop to his target a second thought. Off the eastern tip of the Isle of Wight the signal was given and the *Stukagruppen* began to peel off towards their prearranged targets.

Although some 68 RAF fighters (from Nos 601, 43, 602, 152, 234, 213 and 609 Sqns, plus two Hurricane Is from the FIU) were being vectored towards the approaching aerial armada (whose overall strength totalled four times that number), three of the four *Stukagruppen* were able to carry out their attacks unimpeded by enemy fighters. Only Hauptmann Herbert Meisel's I./StG 77 was intercepted, two squadrons of Hurricanes (Nos 43 and 601) pouncing upon them just as they were manoeuvring into position and about to dive on Thorney Island.

In the space of five minutes ten Stukas, including Meisel's, were shot down, with half as many again being damaged. Of the 56 men that had set out as I./StG 77 from Caen earlier that afternoon, some 17 were killed or mortally wounded (Meisel included), five had been made PoWs and six had returned to France with wounds.

Some 25 kilometres to the east, II./StG 77's devastating attack on Ford faced no aerial opposition. This airfield suffered heavier casualties than the three other targets combined – two hangars, the M/T park, fuel and oil tanks, stores and many other buildings were demolished, 39 aircraft damaged – 13 beyond repair – and 28 personnel killed. It was not until the Stukas were crossing back over the coast near Bognor that they were hit by the 12 Spitfire Is of No 602 Sqn that had scrambled late from Westhampnett. Two of the Ju 87s were immediately sent down into the Channel, whilst two others were damaged – one force-landed on a golf course outside Littlehampton and the other crashed near Barfleur, after struggling back to France. Losses would have been much higher had it not been for the timely intervention of the escorts from JG 27, who rapidly reduced the Spitfire squadron's complement by four.

Just across the River Arun from Ford, Poling CH radar station was the target for Major Bode's III./StG 77. His unit also attacked without hindrance from enemy fighters, but then they too ran into No 602 Sqn as they exited over Bognor in the wake of II. *Gruppe*. A single Stuka was shot

A flying instructor before the war, Helmut Bode first served as a maritime reconnaissance pilot before joining the Stuka arm. He commanded III./StG 77 from its formation in 1940 until August 1942, and is portrayed here with the rank of major later in the war, wearing the Knight's Cross awarded in October 1941

Bringing up the rear of StG 77's formation on 18 August was I.*Gruppe*, commanded by Hauptmann Herbert Meisel. Assigned to attack Thorney Island, this unit lost ten Stukas to defending RAF fighters – Meisel's machine was shot into the sea off Selsey Bill

down (by 7-kill ace Sgt Basil Whall, who had also got a II.*Gruppe* machine just minutes earlier – but not before Unteroffizier Schwemmer, who was manning the aircraft's flexible 7.9 mm MG 15 machine gun, had succeeded in damaging the Spitfire's engine prior to crashing to his death, along with his pilot Unteroffizier Moll, into the sea off Little-hampton. Although Whall managed a more successful forced landing just off the beach at Bognor Regis, he too was subsequently killed in action on 7 October 1940. Of the three damaged Stukas, one crashed in France killing both its crew.

Only the westernmost I./StG 3, targeting Gosport, succeeded in per-formed its attack without interference from the defenders.

As the Ju 87s escaped south over the Channel, gone was the rigid, massed, wingtip to wingtip formation which had so impressed onlookers from the ground during its approach. Now, all was a kaleidoscope of indi-vidual impressions as small groups raced for the haven of France;

'. . . suddenly enemy fighters are upon us. The light haze had hidden them until the last moment. We tuck in closer to the *Staffelkapitän* to concentrate our defensive fire. Above the racket of the guns I hear a loud yell: "Fighter right behind us!" A quick glance to the rear and I see the Spitfire banking away. I also see my wireless-operator, badly wounded, slumped over his gun . . .'

'. . . more *Engländer*. This time we're for it – hit after hit. The wings are shredded, the canopy shattered, my machine-gun mounting jammed. My pilot's voice in the headphones: "Engine and radiator damaged. I'm climbing, prepare to bail out!" White clouds of smoke from the engine. Attacked by two more fighters. One pass – luckily just a few more bullet holes in the wings – and then they break off. Safe for the time being . . .'

'. . . back out to sea at low level. Our *Staffel* bringing up the rear. Two Spitfires take turns at me. Violent manoeuvres to upset their aim. My machine brushes the surface of the water, but recovers. In ten long min-utes we suffer numerous hits. I don't realise until later that I've been slightly wounded too. . .'

'. . . fighters and *Zerstörer* (Blenheim IVf twin-engined fighters of No 235 Sqn, Coastal Command, up from Thorney Island, Ed.) attacking us from all sides. A Hurricane right on our tail. Eight guns against one! The aircraft shudders under the hail of bullets and I suddenly realise we're heading for the water. My pilot has been hit! A minor head wound. But I breathe out again, he's got old *Jolanthe* back under control, and keeps her nose pointing south, course straight home . . .'

'. . . I watch two *Engländer* attacking a Ju flying behind us. The wire-less-operator's fire forces one of them to break away. But the other closes in and hits the Stuka's fuel tanks. The machine bursts into flames and crashes into the sea . . .'

'. . . the English coast drops away behind and the attacks begin to slacken off . . .'

'. . . the engine has finally quit. Will we make it? The pilot begins to glide and cautiously lowers the flaps. We are losing height all the time, but the French coast slowly draws closer. And yes, we've done it! A gentle turn towards the beach, and suddenly a loud tearing noise. The fuselage breaks apart just behind me, propeller and undercarriage fly off into the distance, the wings fold up like paper . . .'

A German reconnaissance photograph of Ford airfield, targeted by II./StG 77, shows dense smoke still billowing from the blazing fuel tanks and partially obscuring the winding River Arun. Poling CH radar station, III./StG 77's objective, is on the far side of the river just off to the right of the picture

Ju 87B-1, 'S2+UN' of 5./StG 77, which force-landed on Ham Manor Golf Course at Angmering, near Littlehampton, after the attack on Ford. Both crew members were seriously wounded by fire from the Spitfire I of No 602 Sqn's Sgt Basil Whall – the latter also went on to destroy a III./StG 77 machine, but was himself shot down in the process

'. . . "How much further?" I ask my pilot. "Fifteen minutes!" This quarter of an hour lasts an eternity. I am still losing blood. At last, our home field is in sight. We land heavily and the whole machine judders. Both tyres are shot through. We spin round crazily and then come to a halt. I try to clamber out but can't. I'm too weak and dizzy from loss of blood. It's not until I'm taken into the sick-bay that I realise what a sight I am, covered in blood like a clumsy butcher in a slaughterhouse!'

For StG 77 the final cost of the day's action was 17 aircraft shot down or written off, with a further seven damaged. It ended at a stroke the Stuka's part in the Battle of Britain, and burst the bubble of the fearsome reputation it had built up over Poland and France. And all to little avail, for once again Luftwaffe intelligence had erred – not one of the three airfields attacked had been a Fighter Command station. At Ford, for example, the 13 machines destroyed were made up of a dozen Fleet Air Arm biplanes – five Swordfish, five Sharks and two Albacores!

After the losses of 18 August VIII. *Fliegerkorps* was transferred eastwards to the control of *Luftflotte* 2. Concentrated in the Pas de Calais, they sat out the remainder of the Battle as a sort of aeronautical 'fleet-in-being', posing a threat by their very presence, and serving to indicate to the British that the invasion was imminent. But the reality was very different. In the Battle of France the Stukas did not reach the Swiss border because they had not been required to. In the Battle of Britain they did not venture into middle England because they had not been able to. And when Operation *'Seelöwe'* ('Sea Lion') – the planned cross-Channel invasion – was quietly shelved on Hitler's orders, the bulk of the *Stukagruppen* were retired equally discreetly back to the Homeland.

A number of *Staffeln* did remain in northern France, however, and in the first half of November 1940 they returned to square one by staging a few sporadic anti-convoy missions around the Kent coast. The first of these, on 1 November, was mounted by 20 Ju 87Bs from the St Pol-based StG 1 against shipping in the Straits of Dover and the Thames Estuary. While their JG 26 escort managed to keep RAF fighters (Spitfires from Nos 74 and 92 Sqns) at bay, the Stukas sank two minor RN vessels, but

Arguably the most enduring image of the entire Battle of Britain is this machine, one of Hauptmann Meisel's luckless I./StG 77 whose final moments were caught on film as it plunged to destruction in a farmer's field outside Chichester . . .

. . . the funeral pyre of Unteroffiziers Kohl and Dann signalled the end of the Stuka's participation in the Battle

forfeited one of their own (a 5.*Staffel* machine crewed by Gefreiters W Karrach and M Aulehner, the former being killed in the crash and the latter rescued by RN motor torpedo boat) when its engine was set alight by AA fire from one of the convoy escorts.

Six days later I./StG 3 suffered one aircraft damaged during a raid on shipping in the Thames Estuary, the Stuka's pilot, Leutnant Eberhard Morgenroth, being injured when his Stuka was attacked by No 249 Sqn Hurricane ace Plt Off T F Neil, who was credited with shooting the Ju 87B down. Gunners on the convoy escort HMS *Egret* also claimed to have shot a Stuka down during the course of the attack which saw the 1700-ton merchantman SS *Astrologer* sunk, and another vessel damaged.

A smaller number of Ju 87s from the *Gruppe* also attacked shipping off Portsmouth at around the same time as the Thames Estuary convoy was bombed, although on this occasion no vessels were hit. No 145 Sqn attempted to engage the Stukas, but were effectively driven off by Bf 109Es of I./JG 2, who downed no less than five Hurricanes from the unit in just a matter of minutes – one British pilot managed to evade the escorts and fire a few fleeting bursts at a lone Ju 87, which he claimed to have probably destroyed, but none of the Stukas involved were damaged.

On 8 November I./StG 3 and IV.(St)/LG 1 despatched some forty aircraft each (escorted by I./JG 51) against shipping along the north Kent and Essex coasts. The solitary unit defending the convoy was the Hurricane-equipped No 17 Sqn, scrambled from Martlesham Heath. The veteran pilots weighed into the Ju 87s, avoiding interception by the escorts thanks to the timely arrival of more Hurricanes from Nos 249 and 46 Sqns. Upon returning to their Suffolk base, the No 17 Sqn crews claimed to have destroyed 15 of the raiders, with five aces and the station commander, Wg Cdr A D Farquhar (also an ace), sharing the bulk of the 'kills'. In fact, only three Stukas were lost, two from 3./StG 3 and one from 12./LG 1 – all six crewmen were killed. A fourth Stuka, from 1./StG 3, force-landed at Dunkirk having run out of fuel. No ships were lost, although several were damaged including the destroyer HMS *Winchester*.

After two final raids (on 11 and 14 November over the Thames and the Straits of Dover respectively) had each cost 9./StG 1 a brace of aircraft downed (RAF overclaiming in the aftermath of the second of these raids saw pilots from Nos 66 and 74 Sqns submitting claims for 16 Ju 87s destroyed!) and seven crewmen killed or missing, the Stukas abandoned their daylight attacks on south-east England's inshore shipping lanes.

But in December StG 1 moved up to Ostende, in Belgium, and early in the New Year the Ju 87 embarked upon the last act in its campaign against Great Britain. What was to come was a far cry from the ambitious third, and final, phase of its part in the Battle as had initially been envisaged the previous summer, however. For when, in January 1941, the Stuka reappeared over England, it was not in massed ranks of 'flying artillery' spearheading the invading ground armies' break-out from the Dover-Worthing beachhead towards their first objective (a line drawn from the Medway to the Solent), but singly, never more than three at any one time, and under cover of darkness.

The first reported incursions occurred on the night of 15-16 January when two Stukas each dropped an SC 1000 high-explosive bomb apiece on south-east London, and a third targeted Dover. Forty-eight hours later

THE MYTH IS EXPLODED

another trio raided the capital and two more returned the next night. Bad weather then halted operations. The Stukas next appeared shortly after sunrise on 5 February, an aircraft from 2./StG 1 attacking and sinking the RN trawler *Tourmaline* off the Kent coast, but paying the price by falling victim to a quartet of Spitfires of No 92 Sqn on convoy escort. A witness to this one-sided engagement was the unit's CO, Battle of Britain ace Sqn Ldr Johnny Kent, who observed the Stuka's demise from the ground;

'On one of the many soul-destroying convoy protection patrols undertaken by the squadron in the New Year of 1941, the formation leader was startled to see one of the ships explode; his first thought was that it must have struck a mine but then, to his amazement, he saw one lone Stuka low on the water heading for France. He and the other three dived to the attack, and the German pilot (Leutnant E Schimmelpfennig, with Obergefrieter H Kaden as wireless operator, Ed.), seeing the Spitfires after him, turned and made for Manston, presumably to give himself up, as he had no hope of survival in a fight.

'The night before this episode some of the officers had been saying that if they brought down a German in one piece the thing to do would be to take him to the Mess and entertain him, before bundling him off to a PoW camp. I did not feel that there was any place for the chivalry displayed in the First World War, and I gave the boys a little lecture on the reasons they were there: this boiled down to first defending the country, and secondly to killing as many of the enemy as possible – and they had better get that firmly into their heads. They learned their lesson very well.

'Having been on the first patrol of the morning, I had been back to the Mess for breakfast and was just returning to Dispersal when I heard gunfire. I stopped the car and got out to stare in amazement at the sight of one lone Stuka weaving madly in an attempt to avoid the attentions of four Spitfires. All five were coming towards me, and it occurred to me that I was in the line of fire so I hid behind a vehicle that was handy. Then I saw a notice on it reading "100 Octane" – it was one of the refuelling bowsers, so I darted back to my car! Just as I reached it the Stuka reached the edge of the airfield almost directly above me at about a hundred feet. Here he was headed off by one of the Spitfires and I could clearly see both gunner and pilot in their cockpits with the De Wilde ammunition bursting around them. The Spitfire overshot and pulled away and the German made another desperate attempt to land and turned violently to port, but at this instant Plt Off Fokes (Plt Off R H Fokes, who scored nine kills with this unit, and was eventually killed in action in June 1944, Ed.), in my aeroplane, flashed past me and gave a short burst with the cannons. I can still hear the "thump-thump-thump" of them followed by the terrific "whoosh" as the Stuka blew up and crashed just outside the boundary of the airfield.

'My words had been taken rather too literally, as it would have been

By contrast, arguably the luckiest man of that 18 August was Unteroffizier Karl Maier, a wireless-operator/gunner of I. *Gruppe*, who returned from Thorney Island having been hit by no fewer than eight machine-gun bullets – and lived to tell the tale! Maier is believed to be the author of the account likening himself to a 'clumsy butcher in a slaughterhouse'

The end of the line for most Luftwaffe machines brought down during the Battle of Britain was one or other of the aircraft dumps which dotted southern England. Seen here behind a pair of KG 2 Dornier Do 17 fuselages is Ju 87 T6+HL of 3./StG 2, its national insignia already stripped by souvenir hunters. Could it possibly be the same 'Heinrich-Ludwig' pictured on pages 50-51. What a pity that yellow-tipped spinner with its tell-tale dent is not visible!

better to have let him land; at that time we did not possess an intact Stuka, and it would have been very useful, particularly in setting at rest the minds of those vociferous Members of Parliament who complained so long and so loudly about the fact that the RAF had no comparable dive-bomber, and in so doing gave the Stuka an importance it did not deserve – certainly not in attacks on England.

'The German crew, both of whom were killed, were a very brave, if foolhardy, pair. They had come over alone from their base in Belgium (some reports state that a sec-

ond Ju 87 was also involved in the trawler sinking, but if so, the eagle-eyed quartet of No 92 Sqn pilots failed to see it, Ed.) and bombed and sunk the ship right under the noses of the fighters while they must have known that their chances of getting home were practically non-existent.'

On the night of 11-12 February RN trawler *Eager* avenged her sister's loss by shooting down a 5.*Staffel* aircraft (one of six despatched on the mission) during a nocturnal dive bombing raid on Chatham naval dockyard. And the following night an aircraft of 9.*Staffel* failed to return from another such sortie over the Thames Estuary, although on this occasion no claims were made by the defenders – Feldwebel F Lewandowski and Unteroffizier L Rener simply being posted missing in 'J9+LL'.

This was the last reported loss of a Ju 87 over the United Kingdom. The early wartime career of a machine which had wreaked havoc from Warsaw to Dunkirk thus ended not with a bang, but with a whimper. Yet, even as the dark, wintry, waters of the Thames were closing over the black-bellied 'Berta' of 9./StG 1, the blue skies of the Mediterranean were witnessing a resurgence in the Stuka's fortunes. But that, as may have been said before, is another story . . .

The precise reason for, and location of, this dummy Stuka is not known, but after 18 August there was no need for such subterfuge. There were enough unemployed Ju 87s parked about the Pas de Calais to furnish and equip any and every deception scheme imaginable

Below left
The quartet of No 92 Sqn pilots responsible for the Ju 87 kill on 5 February 1941 admire their handiwork. Plt Off R H Fokes was credited with the kill, and he is seen here with his hand on the underside of the mangled fuselage

Below
A far cry from the massed take-offs of yesteryear as a lone Ju 87 of StG 1 climbs into the evening sky and sets solitary course for England early in 1941

APPENDICES

TECHNICAL SPECIFICATIONS

	Ju 87A-1	**Ju 87B-1**
POWERPLANT:		
	One 640 hp	One 1200 hp
	Junkers Jumo 210Ca	Junkers Jumo 211Da
PERFORMANCE:		
Max speed	320 kmh	340 kmh
Cruising speed	275 kmh	282 kmh
Max range	1000 km	790 km
Service ceiling	7000 m	8000 m
WEIGHTS:		
Empty	2315 kg	2710 kg
Maximum	3400 kg	4340 kg
DIMENSIONS:		
Wing span	13.80 m	13.80 m
Length	10.78 m	11.10 m
Height	3.89 m	4.01 m
Wing area	31.90 m^2	31.90 m^2
ARMAMENT:		
	One fixed forward-firing 7.9 mm machine-gun in starboard wing; one flexible 7.9 mm machine-gun in rear cockpit; max bomb load 250 kg (500 kg as single-seater)	Two fixed forward-firing 7.9 mm machine-guns in wings; one flexible 7.9 mm machine-gun in rear cockpit; max bomb load 500 kg

ORDERS OF BATTLE

POLAND: 1 September 1939

***Luftflotte* 3** (Roth near Nuremberg): Gen der Flieger Hugo Sperrle

6. Fliegerdivision: Generalmajor Otto Dessloch

III./StG 51	Wertheim	Maj von Klitzing	Ju 87B	31-29

***Luftflotte* 1** (Stettin-Henningsholm): Gen der Flieger Albert Kesselring

1. Fliegerdivision: Generalleutnant Ulrich Grauert

II./StG 2	Stolp-Reitz	Haupt Schmidt	Ju 87B	35-34
III./StG 2	Stolp-West	Haupt Ott	Ju 87B	36-34
IV.(St)/LG 1	Stolp-Reitz	Haupt Kögel	Ju 87B	39-37
4.(St)/TrGr 186	Stolp-West	Haupt Blattner	Ju 87B/C	12-12

Luftwaffenkommando Ostpreußen: Generalleutnant Wilhelm Wimmer

I./StG 1	Elbing	Haupt Hozzel	Ju 87B	38-38

***Luftflotte* 4** (Reihenbach/Silesia): Gen der Flieger Alexander Löhr

2. Fliegerdivision: Generalmajor Bruno Loerzer

I./StG 2	Nieder-Ellguth	Maj Dinort	Ju 87B	38-37

Fliegerführer z.b.V: Generalmajor Wolfram *Freiherr* von Richthofen

Stab StG 77	Neudorf	Oberst Schwartzkopff	Ju 87B	3-3
I./StG 77	Ottmuth	Haupt von Dalwigk	Ju 87B	39-34
II./StG 77	Neudorf	Haupt von Schönborn	Ju 87B	39-38
I./StG 76	Nieder-Ellguth	Haupt Sigel	Ju 87B	36-28

NORWAY: 9 April 1940

X.*Fliegerkorps* (Hamburg): Generalleutnant Hans Geissler

I./StG 1	Kiel-Holtenau	Haupt Hozzel	Ju 87R	39-33

THE LOW COUNTRIES AND FRANCE: 10 May 1940

***Luftflotte* 2** (Münster): Gen der Flieger Albert Kesselring

VIII. *Fliegerkorps:* Generalmajor *Freiherr* von Richthofen

Stab StG 2	Cologne-Ostheim	Maj Dinort	Ju 87B	3-3
I./StG 2	Cologne-Ostheim	Haupt Hitschhold	Ju 87B	40-23
III./StG 2	Nörvenich	Maj von Schönborn	Ju 87B	38-27
I./StG 76	Cologne-Ostheim	Haupt Sigel	Ju 87B	39-34
Stab StG 77	Cologne-Butzweilerhof	Oberst Schwartzkopff	Ju 87B	4-3
I./StG 77	Cologne-Butzweilerhof	Haupt von Dalwigk	Ju 87B	39-31
II./StG 77	Cologne-Butzweilerhof	Haupt Plewig	Ju 87B	39-30
IV.(St)/LG 1	Duisburg	Haupt Kösl	Ju 87B	39-37

***Luftflotte* 3** (Bad Orb): Gen der Flieger Hugo Sperrle

I. *Fliegerkorps:* Gen der Flieger Ulrich Grauert

III./StG 51	Cologne-Wahn	Maj von Klitzing	Ju 87B	39-31

II. *Fliegerkorps:* Generalleutnant Bruno Loerzer

Stab StG 1	Siegburg	Oberst Baier	Ju 87B	3-3
II./StG 2	Siegburg	Maj Enneccerus	Ju 87B	38-33
I.(St)/TrGr 186	Hemweiler	Haupt Hagen	Ju 87B	39-36

BATTLE OF BRITAIN: 13 August 1940

***Luftflotte* 2** (Brussels): Generalfeldmarschall Albert Kesselring

II. *Fliegerkorps:* Gen der Flieger Bruno Loerzer

II./StG 1 (III./StG 51)	Norrent-Fontès	Haupt Keil	Ju 87B	38-30
IV.(St)/LG 1	Tramecourt	Haupt von Brauchitsch	Ju 87B	36-28

Luftflotte 3 (Paris): Generalfeldmarschall Hugo Sperrle

VIII. *Fliegerkorps:* Gen der Flieger Wolfram von Richthofen

Stab StG 1	Angers	Maj Hagen	Ju 87B	3-2
I./StG 1	Angers	Maj Hozzel	Ju 87R	39-27
III./StG 1 (I.(St)/TrGr 186)	Angers	Haupt Mahlke	Ju 87B	38-26
Stab StG 2	St Malo	Maj Dinort	Ju 87B	4-3
I./StG 2	St Malo	Haupt Hitschhold	Ju 87B	35-29
II./StG 2	Lannion	Haupt Enneccerus	(Ju 87B	2-2)
			(Ju 87R	37-31)
III./StG 2	-	Haupt Brücker	Ju 87B	-
Stab StG 3	Caen	-	Ju 87B	5-2
I./StG3 (I./StG 76)	Caen	Haupt Sigel	Ju 87B	24-14
Stab StG 77	Caen	Maj von Schönborn	Ju 87B	4-3
I./StG 77	Caen	Haupt Meisel	Ju 87B	36-33
II./StG 77	Caen	-	Ju 87B	37-25
III./StG 77 (II./KG 76)	Caen	Haupt Bode	Ju 87B	38-37

STUKAGESCHWADER KNIGHT'S CROSS RECIPIENTS 1940

		Date of Award	Fate
1	Hozzel, Hauptmann Paul-Werner	8/5/40	
2	Möbus, Leutnant Martin	8/5/40	2/6/44 (+)
3	Schaefer, Oberleutnant Elmar	8/5/40	
4	Grenzel, Unteroffizier Gerhard	8/5/40	10/1/41 (MiA)
5	Dinort, Major Oskar	20/6/40	
6	von Dalwigk zu Lichtenfels, Hauptmann Friedrich-Karl *Freiherr*	21/7/40[*]	9/7/40 (KiA)
7	Enneccerus, Hauptmann Walter	21/7/40	
8	Hagen, Major Walter	21/7/40	
9	Hitschhold, Hauptmann Hubertus	21/7/40	
10	von Schönborn-Wiesentheid, Major Clemens *Graf*	21/7/40	30/8/44 (+)
11	Sigel, Hauptmann Walter	21/7/40	8/5/44 (+)
12	Keil, Hauptmann Anton	19/8/40	29/8/41 (KiA)
13	Brandenburg, Oberleutnant Johannes	18/9/40	28/2/42 (KiA)
14	Schwartzkopff, Oberst Gunther	24/11/40[*]	14/5/40 (KiA)
15	Plewig, Hauptmann Waldemar	14/12/40	8/8/40 (PoW)

[*] posthumous

(+) killed whilst on active service

Generalmajor Wolfram *Freiherr* von Richthofen, GOC VIII.*Fliegerkorps*, was also awarded the Knight's Cross on 18/5/40

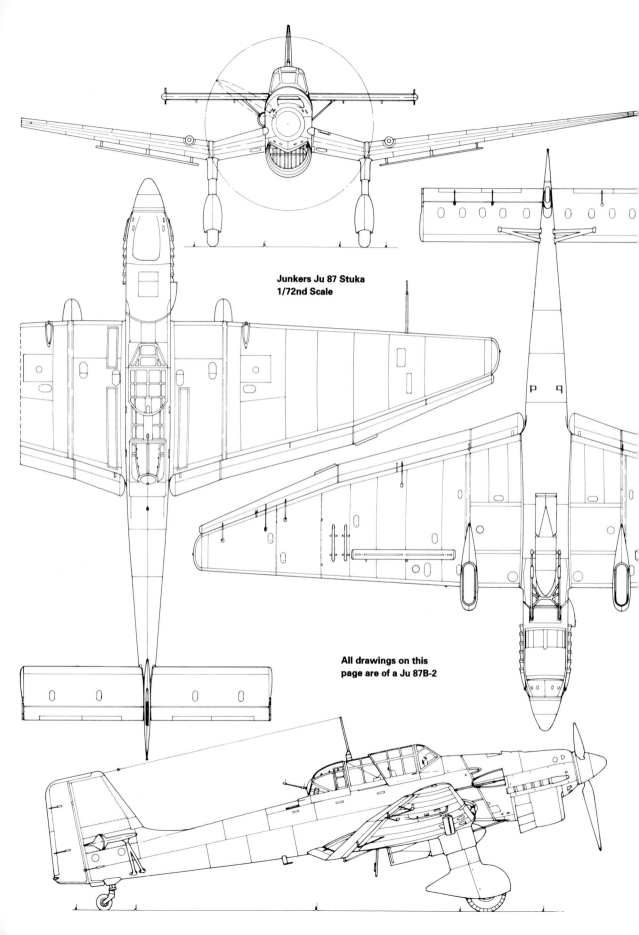

Junkers Ju 87 Stuka
1/72nd Scale

**All drawings on this
page are of a Ju 87B-2**

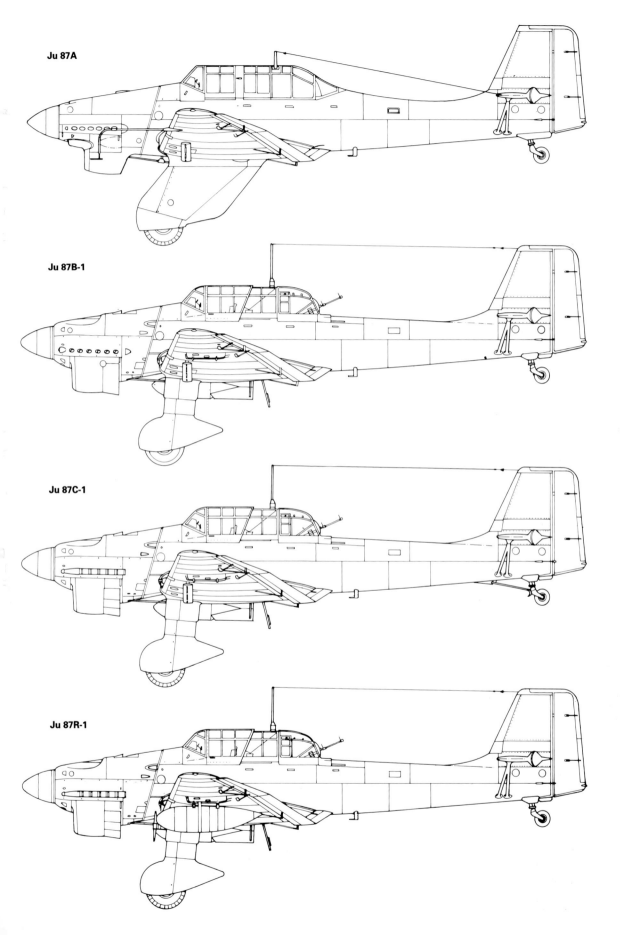

Ju 87A

Ju 87B-1

Ju 87C-1

Ju 87R-1

COLOUR PLATES

1

Ju 87B-1 '35+G12' of 2./StG 163 'Immelmann', Cottbus, February 1939

Apart form the early pre-production models, all 'Bertas' were initially delivered in the standard black-green/dark-green (70/71) finish as shown here. This example still wears the five-part military designation first introduced on 1 June 1936. In this system, the two digits to the left of the fuselage cross indicate, respectively, the *Luftkreiskommando* (local air command) to which the *Geschwader* belonged (3) and the numerical sequence of the *Geschwader* within that *Luftkreis* (5). Immediately to the right of the cross is the aircraft's individual identity code letter (G). This is followed by the *Gruppe* (1) and the *Staffel* (2) digits. Unusually, 2./StG 163 Ju 87s at this time also carried non-military style individual numbers on their cowlings.

2

Ju 87A-1 '35+Y25' of 5./StG 163 'Immelmann', Grottkau/Silesia, January 1939

Recently converted from the Hs 123 on to the Ju 87, II./StG 163's 'Antons' wore the standard early three-colour upper surface camouflage of dark-brown (61), green (62) and grey (63), with light-blue (65) undersides. As part of the second *Staffel* within its particular *Gruppe* (II. *Gruppen* normally consisted of 4., 5. and 6. *Staffeln*), the individual aircraft letter is again red as above. The overpainting of the red band behind the tail swastika puts the date as post-1 January 1939.

3

Ju 87A-1 '52+A12' of 2./StG 165, Pocking, March 1938

Depicted at the time of the annexation of Austria, this machine wears a similar three-tone camouflage to that above, albeit with the colours transposed. Note, however, the red tail band with the swastika superimposed on a white disc – the standard tail marking for all military aircraft between 15 September

1935 and 1 January 1939. Note too the seven-digit *Werk-Nummer* (0870101) immediately below the red band, and the uncommon presentation of both the individual aircraft letter (A) and the *Staffel* designator (2) in white.

4

Ju 87A-1 '81+E11' of 1./StG 168, Graz-Thalerhof, April 1938

After its incorporation into the Greater German Reich, Austria became officially known as the '*Ostmark*'. The only *Stukagruppe* based in the newly-annexed 'Eastern border region' was I./StG 168, represented here by 'E-Emil'.

5

Ju 87A-1 '29.2' of 5.J/88 *Condor Legion*, Vitoria/Spain, January 1938

One of the original trio of A-1s sent to Spain at the beginning of 1938, '29.2' displays standard three-tone Luftwaffe camouflage with Nationalist Spanish insignia applied, the latter consisting of a solid black fuselage disc, a diagonal black cross on the white rudder and reversed wing markings of a white cross on a black disc. Note too the white wingtips.

6

Ju 87A-1 '29.4' of 5.J/88 *Condor Legion* Calamocha/Spain, February 1938

Almost identical in appearance to the previous machine except for its individual aircraft number, 29.4 was the mount of Leutnant Hermann Haas – the first *Kettenführer* of 5.J/88 – and his wireless-operator/gunner, Feldwebel Emil Kramer. Now unofficially, but universally, known as the 'Jolanthe-*Kette*', 29.4 sports the famous pink pig badge on its undercarriage trousers, the lower fairings of which have been re-moved to improve take-off and landing runs across Calamocha's soft and sandy surface.

7

Ju 87B-1 '29.6' of 5.J/88 *Condor Legion*,

Catalonia/Spain, January 1939

The 'Antons' were replaced by 'Bertas' late in 1938. The newcomers also combined standard Luftwaffe camouflage – now the new two-tone green – with Nationalist Spanish markings as depicted here. Although attached to the *'Legion's* bomber wing, several of the 'Bertas' continued to wear the orginal 'Jolanthe-*Kette'* emblem on their wheelspats.

8
Ju 87B-1 'A5+AB' of *Stab* I./StG 1, Elbing/East Prussia, September 1939

Presumably the aircraft of Hauptmann Paul-Werner Hozzel, *Gruppenkommandeur* of I./StG 1, this machine displays the new unit fuselage code markings introduced at the time of the major redesignation programme in the early summer of 1939 – a combination of letter and numeral to the left of the fuselage cross denoting the *Geschwader* (StG 1's code being 'A5'), with the individual aircraft letter again immediately to the right of the cross, and the fourth and final letter representing the particular *Stab* or *Staffel* within the *Geschwader* to which the machine belonged. 'B' indicated the *Stab* of I.*Gruppe*, and was more usually applied in green rather than the white shown here. Note also the *Kommandeur's* fuselage band immediately aft of the cockpit canopy and the *Gruppe* badge on the wheelspat.

9
Ju 87B-1 'A5+FH' of 1./StG 1, Elbing/East Prussia, September 1939

Very similar to the *Kommandeur's* machine (but with the *Geschwader* code now on an even keel!), 1. *Staffel's* 'Friedrich-Heinrich' displays the *Gruppe* badge in its more common position below the windscreen. This emblem was a stylised representation of one 'Hans Huckebein', a naughty raven – a sort of 19th century German Mickey Mouse – created by early cartoonist Wilhelm Busch.

10
Ju 87R 'A5+CL' of 3./StG 1, Stavanger-Sola/Norway, April 1940

The long-range Ju 87Rs with which I./StG 1 re-equipped early in 1940 featured the revised national markings introduced after the Polish campaign – fuselage crosses with broader (higher visibility) white outlines and tail swastikas moved forward from the rudder hinge line on to the tailfin. The 'Diving Raven' *Gruppe* badge has also moved forward to the engine cowling.

11
Ju 87B-1 '6G+LT' of 6./StG 1, Norrent-Fontès/France, August 1940

When StG 1 was brought up to full *Geschwader* status in July 1940 the second *Gruppe* slot was filled by redesignating the erstwhile III./StG 51. For some time after assuming their new identity the aircraft of II./StG 1 retained both their old *Gruppe* badge (a torch-bearing devil astride a bomb) and their previous fuselage codes, as witness 'Ludwig-Theodor' here – an ex-9./StG 51 machine which also displays the somewhat unusual combination of new style fuselage cross with tail swastika still in the pre-1940 location across the rudder hinge line.

12
Ju 87B-2 'J9+IH' of 7./StG 1, Ostende/Belgium, January 1941

III./StG 1 had previously been I.(St)/TrGr 186, and this *Gruppe* too retained its previous unit codes long after its redesignation in July 1940. The temporary black undersides and overpainting of all white markings and insignia point to 'Ida-Heinrich's' participation in the nocturnal attacks on south-east England early in 1941, although the retention of the unit badge – a winged helmet superimposed on an anchor, as befitting its ex-naval background – did somewhat compromise these precautions. Many aircraft of this *Gruppe* also carried the names of previous actions on their engine cowlings including 'Boulogne' and 'Lee-on-Solent'.

13
Ju 87B-1 'T6+CA' of *Stab* StG 2 'Immelmann', Cologne-Ostheim, May 1940

A standard finish B-1 of the *Geschwaderstab* StG 2 'Immelmann' in French campaign markings, complete with new enlarged underwing crosses. Photographic evidence seems to suggest that the *Stabskette* badge was initially presented as a black cross on a white shield before the colours were reversed as shown here, only to revert to black on white again later in the war! Note the small propellers on the undercarriage leg fairings. These were intended to add an extra dimension of terror by emitting an unearthly howl during the dive, but were soon removed by most units because of their adverse effect on the Stuka's already marginal performance in level flight.

14
Ju 87B-2 'T6+KH' of 1./StG 2 'Immelmann', Cologne-Ostheim, May 1940

All I./StG 2 aircraft were initially distinguished by their prominent *Gruppe* badge. Modelled on Major Hitschhold's pet scottie 'Molch', this was carried on a disc in the respective *Staffel* colours – white for 1./StG 2. Also in white are the spinner tip, the nose cap of the propeller fairing on the under-carriage leg (with the offending propeller already removed!) and the individual letter 'K', repeated on the front of each wheelspat.

15
Ju 87B-2 'T6+HL' of 3./StG 2 'Immelmann', St Malo/France, August 1940

Otherwise identical to 1.*Staffel*'s 'Kurfürst-Heinrich', this machine wears the yellow trim and the code letter 'L' of 3./StG 2. Note too that although retaining the yellow disc (which presumably once carried the *Gruppe*'s scottie-dog emblem), 3.*Staffel* at some stage chose to go their own way, opting instead for the coat-of-arms of the city of Breslau, their home station back in 1937.

16
Ju 87B-2 'T6+GM' of 4./StG 2 'Immelmann', Siegburg, May 1940

Unlike I.*Gruppe*, the component *Staffeln* of II./StG 2 each had their own individual badge from the outset, that of 4.*Staffel* being the lucky four-leaf clover depicted here. This machine also combines a new-style fuselage cross with pre-1940 positioned tail swastika. Note the small 'screamers' attached to the fins of the underwing bombs. Fashioned out

of cardboard and shaped like miniature organ pipes, they were another device intended to spread panic among troops being subjected to Stuka attack – old bayonet scabbards with notches cut in them were also sometimes used. The Luftwaffe christened these screamers *'Jericho-Trompeten'* – 'Trumpets of Jericho'!

17
Ju 87B-2 'T6+KN' of 5./StG 2 'Immelmann', Lannion/France, August 1940

A regulation set of markings – swastika correctly located on the tailfin – for 5.*Staffel*'s 'Kurfürst-Nordpol', together with the unit's 'aggressive penguin' badge below the windscreen and the individual aircraft letter 'K' in black, thinly outlined in red.

18
Ju 87B-1 'T6+RT' of 9./StG 2 'Immelmann', Nörvenich, May 1940

III./StG 2's *Staffeln* also favoured individual emblems. Here, the 'dancing devil' on the yellow shield, plus the yellow spinner tip and individual aircraft letter, carried in conjunction with the *Staffel* code letter 'T', all point conclusively to 9./StG 2.

19
Ju 87B-1 'S7+NL' of 3./StG 3, Caen/France, August 1940

The only *Stukagruppe* to have been stationed in pre-war Austria, I./StG 76 must have retained a certain sense of isolation even after its redesignation as I./StG 3 immediately prior to the Battle of Britain, for the other two *Gruppen* of the embryonic StG 3 were not created until 1942! Known as the 'Graz *Gruppe*' since its earliest days as I./StG 168, this unit also selected the coat-of-arms of its home town as its identifying badge.

20
Ju 87B-2 '6G+CD' of *Stab* III./StG 51, Cologne-Wahn, May 1940

Another example of new-style fuselage cross combined with a tail swastika overlapping both fin and rudder, 'Cäsar-Dora' also illustrates this *Geschwaderstab*'s unusual presentation of its unit codes – variously described as pale grey or (more likely) light green – during the campaign in France. The *Gruppenstab* badge is another geographical reference, depicting the 'Eagle of Tyrol'.

21
Ju 87B-1 '6G+FR' of 7./StG 51, France, June 1940
Perhaps the most flamboyant of all Stuka unit emblems of the early war years, 7./StG 51's badge combined a charging bull on a yellow star background beneath the windscreen, with a yellow comet tail stretching back almost the entire length of the cockpit canopy.

22
Ju 87B-1 'S2+AH' of 1./StG 77, Caen-Maltot/France, August 1940
StG 77 had arguably the most regimented system of unit badges of any Ju 87 *Gruppe*. Every aircraft in the *Geschwader* bore the same yellow shield with an indented upper field in the respective *Stab* or *Gruppe* colour. Each unit, from *Geschwaderstab* downwards, also had its own device on the main body of the shield – in the case of I.*Staffel* this was a leaping pig. The individual aircraft letter 'A' identifies this as the machine of the *Staffelkapitän*, Oberleutnant Trogemann.

23
Ju 87B-1 'S2+EM' of 4./StG 77, Cologne-Butzweilerhof, May 1940
Conforming to *Geschwader* regulations, this otherwise perfectly standard B-1 features the unit badge with a red upper segment indicating II.*Gruppe* and *Staffel* emblem of a crowing cockerel. Note that the fairing for the propeller siren on 'Emil-Martha's' undercarriage leg has been capped off by a flat plate.

24
Ju 87B-1 'S2+NN' of 5./StG 77, Neudorf, September 1939
Another II.*Gruppe* machine as witness the red trim, this B-1 carries standard early wartime markings and the 5.*Staffel* badge of the Polish campaign period. This latter emblem consisted of a hare, wearing a Polish army cap, about to be hit by a bomb.

25
Ju 87B-2 'F1+AC' of *Stab* III./StG 77, Caen/France, August 1940
Unable to use yellow for the upper segment of their badges, III./StG 77 elected for blue instead. The *Gruppenstab* emblem on the main yellow field was a knight on horseback, the family crest of the *Kommandeur* Hauptmann Helmuth Bode – certain members of the *Stab* unkindly suggested that the insignia on the knight's shield, three yellow stars and a yellow disc, stood for three-star brandy and a glass of beer viewed from above!

26
Ju 87B-2 'F1+DP' of 9./StG 77, Caen/France, August 1940
Very similar overall to Bode's Stuka, the aircraft of 9.*Staffel* featured a far less imaginative badge. They selected as their emblem a diving eagle clutching a bomb in its talons. Note, however, that all Ju 87s of III./StG 77, including both 'Anton-Cäsar' and 'Dora-Paula', initially retained the fuselage codes of the unit from which they were formed – the Do 17-equipped II./KG 76.

27
Ju 87B-1 'L1+JW' of 12.(St)/LG 1, Stolp-Reitz, September 1939
Wearing standard markings for the early months of the war (thin-edged fuselage cross and tail swastika on the rudder hinge line), this B-1 is identifiable solely by its fuselage code, IV.(St)/LG 1's *Gruppe* badge not yet having been applied.

28
Ju 87B-1 'J9+TM' of 4.(St)/TrGr 186, Stolp-West, September 1939
Operating as a single *Staffel* during the Polish campaign, the aircraft of 4.(St)/TrGr 186 featured a badge reflecting their naval aviation status – an anchor and winged helmet. They retained both badge and unit code 'J9' for much of their subsequent wartime career as part of III./StG 1.

29
Ju 87A-2 'S13+S29' of an unidentified training unit, Nuremberg area, circa early 1939

Back briefly to a three-tone camouflaged 'Anton' as flown at an unidentified training school during the months leading up to the war. Although superficially similar to operational unit codes of the same period, the fuselage markings on trainers did differ in some respects. To the left of the fuselage cross, the first 'S' stood for *Schule* (school), the following digit(s) indicating the territorial command area in which the school was situated (in this instance *Luftgaukommando* XIII Nürnberg). The letter immediately to the right of the cross (confusingly in this case another 'S') identified the training flight within the school, and it was the closing digit(s) – here 'White 29' – which provided the aircraft's individual identity.

30
Ju 87B-1 'Yellow A/NO+HP' of FFS(C) 12, Prague-Ruzyne, 1941

In contrast, and representative of ex-operational aircraft relegated to training duties after the outbreak of war, this 'Berta', once of III./StG 2 (note the Hlinka Cross *Gruppe* badge), and now serving with *Fliegerführerschule* (C)12 (Advanced Training School 12) at Prague, has reverted to a four-letter code (possibly its original *Stammkennzeichen* – the basic identity code allocated to each aircraft upon manufacture), augmented by a yellow 'A' for in-school identification.

Figure Plates

1
Oberleutnant Bruno Dilley, *Staffelkapitän* of 3./StG 1 is seen wearing the multi-zippered summer flying suit and early-style kapok life-jacket as used in 1939-40. Note also the officer's field cap (*Fliegermütze*) and cloth patch on his right sleeve denoting rank. Dilley survived the war having flown some 650 combat missions.

2
Leutnant Hermann Haas was the *Kettenführer* of the original trio of Ju 87s sent to Spain, and he is shown here in *Condor Legion* dress and standard Luftwaffe flying boots of the period. The two stars of a '*Teniente*' are worn on his cap and left breast (all Luftwaffe personnel were promoted one rank during their period of service in Spain), whilst the Nationalist flying badge is displayed on the right breast – the whole being set off with sunglasses and holstered Walther 7.65 mm P.P. pistol.

3
After commanding I./StG 2 'Immelmann' in Poland, Major Oskar Dinort served as *Geschwaderkommodore* of StG 2 from October 1939 through to October 1941. Well-known throughout the Luftwaffe, 'Uncle Oskar' also survived the war, latterly as the CO of a training division. Here he wears an outfit similar to Dilley's, albeit with flying helmet, throat microphone and later style inflatable life-jacket. Note also the cloth rank patch.

4
The first NCO of the entire Luftwaffe to be awarded the Knight's Cross (on 8/5/40), Unteroffizier Gerhard Grenzel of I./StG 1 wears a standard issue flying blouse (*Fliegerbluse*) with leather helmet and other ranks' belt, plus obligatory Walther 7.65 mm P.P. pistol. Note Unteroffizier collar patches and shoulder straps. Grenzel failed to return from an attack on a Malta convoy on 10/1/41.

5
Oberst Günther Schwartzkopff, *Geschwaderkommodore* of StG 77, was killed in action over France on 14/5/40. He too is wearing summer flying overalls, but combines these with officer's service cap and belt. Note the Oberst's rank patch prominently displayed on his right sleeve.

6
Schwartzkopff's successor at the head of StG 77 was Major Clemens Graf von Schönborn-Wiesentheid (ex-*Kommandeur* of III./StG 2). Shown in full officer's service dress, he is wearing the Knight's Cross awarded on 21 July 1940. After leading StG 77 in the Balkans and Russia, von Schönborn-Wiesentheid was appointed chief of the Luftwaffe mission in Bulgaria, where he was killed in the crash of a Fieseler *Storch* on 30 August 1944.